DISRUPTION AND HOPE

DISRUPTION AND HOPE

*Religious Traditions
and the
Future of Theological Education*

Essays in Honor of Daniel O. Aleshire

BAYLOR UNIVERSITY PRESS

Unless otherwise stated, Scripture quotations are from
the New Revised Standard Version Bible, copyright 1989,
Division of Christian Education of the National Council
of the Churches of Christ in the United States of America.
Used by permission. All rights reserved.

Cover Design by Alyssa Stepien

Baylor University Press thanks the
Henry Luce Foundation, and especially Michael Gilligan,
whose support made this book possible.

The Library of Congress has cataloged this book under
ISBN 978-1-4813-0815-1.

Printed in the United States of America on acid-free paper
with a minimum of 30 percent recycled content.

CONTENTS

INTRODUCTION
Barbara G. Wheeler

D avid Kelsey, professor of theology and seasoned observer of theological education, once remarked that the impulse to revise curriculum overtakes theological school faculty "with almost seasonal regularity." In prosperous times, the driver of these efforts is usually an educational idea. A group of influential faculty members become convinced that a new pedagogical approach, such as a more substantial core curriculum or a focus on competency, will greatly improve the quality of education. In periods of scarcity, necessity is most often the motive. Educational arrangements that attract more students and cost less to implement are the goal.

The essays in this volume propose an alternative starting point: the theological tradition in which a school stands. Six authors examine the role of traditions amid severe disruptions in the religious and educational environment, a "maelstrom," according to one author, that has imperiled the existence of some schools and put most others under heavy pressures. All the authors recognize the need to contend with these disruptive forces, but only after a long look, both appreciative and critical, at the core commitments that have anchored their schools from the beginning.

David Tiede, who had a long tenure as president of Luther Seminary, states the tradition of Lutheran seminaries in terms of the core doctrines that these schools embrace across lines of differences among Lutheran denominations: "What serves Christ," a bedrock Lutheran theme that encompasses both "justification by faith through grace" and "Christian freedom to serve the neighbor." Tiede recognizes that these motifs have different resonances than they did half a millennium ago, when Martin Luther produced his iconic theses, but the call to conversion, *metanoia*, to the service of Christ has persisted through time. Tiede catalogs the many unsettling developments that make this a "time for turning" and the major changes in institutional form and location that these developments have already created in the Lutheran seminary world. He insists, however, that despite what may appear to be institutional "decompensation," the disruptions are in fact impelling Lutheran schools toward "a more faithful future." The education of the faithful and their leaders to be "little Christs" (Luther's phrase) in this future will, however, require more than technical adjustments to meet current conditions. It must be newly and deeply affirmative of Lutherans' central theological affirmations. "The hopeful way forward," writes Tiede, "is by faith in God's promises."

Martha Horne, the long-serving emeritus president of a seminary of the Episcopal Church, Virginia Theological Seminary, enumerates the theologically grounded practices that constitute the Anglican tradition in which her school stands: its treatment of Scripture as both central and open to a wide range of interpretations, the worldwide reach of its communion, the binding power of liturgy in the church's life together, and its outward focus on mission. Historically, threaded through these ways of life has been "a reluctance to be threatened by differences" and a conviction that "people of good faith may disagree," both contained in the watchword "Anglican comprehensiveness." Like Tiede, Horne offers an inventory of numerous signs of challenge and religious decline, enough to amount, in her words, to "a perfect storm." To fulfill their purposes in such conditions, Horne argues, Anglican schools must both maintain and renew their long-standing habits and practices. Because the center of the Anglican and broader Christian world has shifted from the once-dominant West to a wide range of cultures in the global south, it will take "cross-cultural aptitude" in the reading and interpretation of Scripture to maintain the cohesion of the worldwide communion of Anglican churches. Liturgy will continue to function as the tie that binds the tradition and the communion, but students need to be trained to bring new liturgical "deftness" and flexibility to the task of incorporating a wider range of cultural patterns than have infused Anglican worship in the past. Finally, in a deeply and often murderously divided world, the "openness to differences" that has been the hallmark of Anglican comprehensiveness may be the major missional contribution of Anglican and Episcopal churches and the leaders they educate.

Donald Senior, who accepted the presidency of a Roman Catholic seminary, the Catholic Theological Union, not once but twice for substantial periods of service, illustrates one of the complexities of using "tradition" as a touchstone for rethinking the work of theological schools: within a major tradition, there are multiple strands or subtraditions. Alasdair MacIntyre, cited in David Tiede's contribution, characterized a tradition as an "argument" over which goods should comprise the tradition. Different subtraditions offer different conclusions to the argument. Which of these should ground the identity of the school is a matter for discernment. Roman Catholic preparation of priests and other religious leaders has an overarching unity. It is primarily structured by *Pastores Dabo Vobis*, a statement by Pope John Paul II that identifies four "dimensions" of formation: human, spiritual, intellectual, and pastoral. In the United States and around the world, bishops have used this template to direct theological education in their domains. The dimensions can, however, be inflected in very different ways. Most faithful in present circumstances, Senior believes, is the vision of the current pope, Francis, as expressed in his writings and actions. The "enduring biblical and Christian" themes of this vision—the reconciling "joy of the Gospel," care for creation, and merciful "joy of love"—are, Senior avers,

3

"countercultural," a necessary corrective that "runs contrary to the implied portrayal of humanity" that is widely prevalent today. To implement the vision, seminaries will have to cultivate in their students empathy at the human level, a deep relationship to Christ, an "eye for beauty" in the natural world and the arts, a heart for the poor, and most of all, mercy, which in Francis's words is "the beating heart of the Gospel." These emphases, on tenderness, spiritual depth, sensitivity, kindness, and patience, as well as intellectual acuity, have an honored place in Roman Catholic tradition, though they have not always been prominent. To serve today's and tomorrow's church, however, Senior believes they determine the "tenor" of the work theological schools.

Richard Mouw, former president of Fuller Seminary, looks squarely at some negative facets of tradition. He begins his essay by recounting the long history and current state of a tradition in American evangelicalism that theological educators have struggled to disown: antipathy toward the intellectual life in general and graduate-level seminary training in particular. These attitudes, he reports, are resurgent today, often appearing in tandem with an interest in technical knowledge (marketing, management) and popular culture that—in the view of church leaders who discourage seminary attendance—aid in attracting "seekers" with limited religious backgrounds. Mouw admits his initial inclination to ignore the antiseminary contingent. Local and practical training schools in the past either disappeared or developed into seminaries. But the needs of the present day are too pressing, he concludes, simply to "wait out" the antiseminary movement. Important as it is to promote institutions of higher learning that "take thick confessional traditions seriously," it is even more important, according to Mouw, to engage in a process of thinking and feeling with the church, his translation of *sentire cum ecclesia*. And that requires careful listening to those suspicious of or averse to higher theological education, to understand what fuels their perspective and what challenges they believe other resources will help them address. Mouw, who believes that a "sense of the divine" is built in to human beings along with the tendency to misdirect it, makes a critical point about tradition. Even the undersides of our traditions, the parts of them that are misguided or wrong, can—if approached from a posture of inquiry and genuine interest—"teach us how the yearning of the spirit gets expressed in our contemporary context."

All four of these authors write in the context of major changes in theological education, captured in the title of this book as "disruption." Some of these changes have threatened the stability of theological schools: declining participation in organized religion, lower educational expectations for religious leadership, and rising costs in all educational sectors are the most prominent corrosive trends. Other developments, such as the fast-increasing racial and ethnic diversity of American Christianity and the explosive growth of Christian churches in the global south are full of promise but require North American theological schools to refit what has been a largely white and Anglo enterprise, very much oriented to theological developments in the West. The remaining two authors focus on another major change: the increasing salience of non-Christian traditions in North America. North Americans used to be able to choose whether to travel to encounter other traditions or to stay at home in a largely Christian society. No longer. Because of immigration and a loosening of ascriptive religious ties by birth, it is virtually inevitable that North American Christians will encounter the religious other.

Douglas McConnell, who has served as provost of Fuller Seminary and participant in a project of encounter with other religious traditions, explores the tension, inevitable for evangelical schools and many others, that arises between the need to witness to the truth of one's own, firmly held religious faith and respectful engagement with persons of other faiths. Now that accrediting standards require theological schools to "engage students with . . . multifaith and multicultural" contexts, schools must capacitate students to deal with this tension. McConnell argues that "joyful" witnessing is less likely to be perceived as an imposition on a person of another tradition and may even be received as a "gift." At the same time, education in evangelism must emphasize respect and "convicted civility."

McConnell suggests that it is the duty of theological schools not only to teach the importance of these concepts but also to assess whether their students have actually acquired the habits of respect and civility. He quotes one of his students to express his own resolution of the tension he describes: Christians must be "exclusivist" in their conviction of the centrality of the cross and at the same time "make room for the other in . . . heart and . . . mind."

Judith Berling, an Episcopalian who has taught East Asian religions for her whole career while also serving as dean of the Graduate Theological Union, makes two further contributions to an understanding of how traditions should function to orient theological schools. First, she argues, engagement with other traditions, through study, participant observation, and interpersonal encounters, is likely to show that traditions that have swum in the same "cultural soup" have features in common. That experience offers a "conceptual challenge" to the "notion of a tightly bound, neat, isolated" tradition, a challenge that frees adherents from the straitjacket of a univocal, oversimplified version of their tradition that excludes or negates other traditions. Second, Berling points out that it may be easier to see in traditions other than one's own the wide internal diversity they contain. Indeed, in some sense, each person committed to "a tradition" constructs that tradition somewhat differently. With the freedom to view a theological school's tradition as related to as much as distinct from others comes a capacity to adapt programs to rapidly changing social and religious conditions. With the recognition that one's own and other traditions are far from internally uniform comes the opportunity to educate students to bridge deep social and religious divides by engaging "specific persons" rather than "entire traditions" in the abstract.

Of what practical use are the essays that form this book for a school that wants or needs to revise its curriculum and operating patterns in the light of current conditions? The writers, some of the longest-serving colleagues of Daniel Aleshire, whom the volume honors, represent only a handful of the many traditions that anchor North American theological schools. The Baptist denomination in which Dan grew up; the Methodist Church in which he currently serves; and historically black churches, charismatic churches, immigrant churches, Eastern Orthodox denominations, and many more that belong to the Association of Theological schools would all emphasize very different themes and motifs in their traditions. Very likely, even schools that stand in the same tradition as the authors' will express those traditions somewhat differently. So the writers' analyses and prescriptions are not directly applicable to other institutions.

These essays will prove most helpful if they are used as examples of exercises that schools can conduct for themselves. Taken together, the contributions to this book suggest a syllabus of questions that any schools, including those very different from the authors', might take up. A school that decides to begin its project of revision and adjustment by getting to the heart of the matter—discerning the core identity and mission of the institution—might address these questions. Perhaps each question could be assigned to a different discussion leader, who might use the essay that generates the question as an example of how to proceed. The questions and the authors whose work suggests them are these:

1. **What theological doctrines or affirmations are central to the identity of your institution?** (David Tiede identifies the theological core that he thinks animates the work of Lutheran institutions. Denominational institutions can draw on extensive literatures that explore the theological foundations of their particular group. Schools that serve religious communities of multiple denominations may have to spend considerable time surfacing the theological convictions that hold the school together.)

2. **What practices and patterns of life together are deeply engrained in your school's tradition?** (Martha Horne outlines the theologically based practices that are marks of Anglican tradition. Again, schools related to a single tradition may find it easier to address this question, but all

schools develop habits and ways of life around which they
cohere.)

3. **Within your school's larger tradition, what strands or
   subtraditions does your institution choose to emphasize?**
   (Donald Senior proposes a focus on the "countercultural"
   vision of Pope Francis, a vision grounded in tradition, but
   one of many possible emphases in contemporary Catholicism. Other traditions also have multiple strands, one of
   which dominates an institution's culture.)

4. **What features of your school's tradition has it disowned
   or opposed in the past? Are there lessons to be learned
   from careful listening to opponents within your tradition?** (Richard Mouw illustrates how to resist unhealthy
   tendencies in one's tradition while learning from those who
   hold different or opposing views.)

5. **How does your school aim to balance witness to its core
   beliefs and hospitality to other traditions?** (Douglas
   McConnell makes a strong case from an evangelical perspective for the possibility of incorporating both emphases
   into the formation of students. Other institutions might
   define their nonnegotiable core differently, but all face the
   same challenge.)

6. **What history, themes, and values does your tradition have in common with others? What is the range
   of its internal diversity? How can understanding the
   complexity of your own tradition enable relationships
   with the religious other?** (Judith Berling makes the case
   for appreciating the variety contained within traditions and
   their long-standing relationships to other traditions.)

Tradition, in the various ways that these authors have urged that
it be honored and examined critically, is of course not the only deter-
minant of a school's mission for the future. Each author, as already
noted, devotes plenty of attention to the disruptive changes in the
religious, social, and economic environment that are forcing nearly

every theological school to rethink both its form and its functions. But important as these developments are in setting the stage for revision and renewal, they should not—these writers suggest—be the first or highest considerations as new institutional forms and educational directions are contemplated. Rather, the affirmations and values that have guided the school in the past should be evaluated first to discern which, given the demands of the Gospel in our day, should be retained, restated, or left behind. That discernment will provide a basis for deciding how faithfully to accommodate the strenuous pressures that bear down on theological schools. The outcome of these efforts will be practical wisdom—workable institutional arrangements and educational offerings that are faithful to the One who calls us and that offer hope, not just for our schools and churches, but also for the suffering world they serve.

Daniel O. Aleshire served the Association of Theological Schools (ATS) for close to three decades, two of them as executive director. Michael Gilligan, Dan's associate at ATS for many years and now president of the Henry Luce Foundation, which sponsored the publication of this volume, noted that the theme of the book "is precisely at the heart of Dan's achievement." As director of accreditation at ATS, Dan was always alert to "the specificity of a school's tradition." Gilligan says that Dan "tutored" him and other staff members in those traditions and that he continued to celebrate this specificity in the hundreds of presentations he made over the years to faculty and boards of trustees of member schools and to participants in ATS programs and meetings.

Several of the contributors offered further remarks about the relationship of the themes of this volume to Dan's extraordinary leadership of theological education in North America.

Dan has functioned, wrote Martha Horne, as "the *pater familias* of a large family of theological schools." He has been an advocate for these schools, representing their interests in the wider world of higher education and voicing their needs and aspirations to supporting both church bodies and government regulators. Most significantly, he has presided over and enabled the expansion of the association's membership. On his watch, significant numbers of evangelical schools and newly formed institutions serving immigrant churches have applied to join. As a result, as he retires, ATS is the broadest-based Christian organization in the world, counting among its members Roman Catholic, Eastern Orthodox, mainline and evangelical Protestant, and Unitarian institutions. Dan's "ability to understand and respect the unique expression of this highly diverse group of schools, valuing each of them for their distinctive contributions to . . . the mission of the church" has been a major factor in this development. He has also worked hard to link theological education in North America to theological schools around the world and to encourage theological educators to take educational account of the increasing presence of non-Christian traditions in their own settings. Thus a book that represents multiple Christian traditions and their relationship to other religious communities seems a fitting tribute.

The focus on tradition is appropriate for another reason as well. Though Dan mastered the nuances, details, and technical dimensions of the work of theological schools, he consistently gave even more weight to matters of vocation and mission. His Director's Reports to biennial meetings of ATS served as a reminder of the schools' ultimate purposes. David Tiede described some of these presentations: "[One] featured a photographic essay on the ATS [schools] at worship, peering into the beautiful breadth of doxologies at theological schools, from academic New England chapels, to Pentecostal praise, to liturgies of word and sacrament, to resounding black choirs, to Orthodox incense. Another biennial presentation reported on his visits to the transformations of Christian communities in his native Ohio, bringing the cultural and religious realities of a new era into our shared vision."

One of Dan's regular themes in these reports was the ways that immigrant religious groups and the theological communities of other people of color were remaking the churches and infusing them and the schools that serve them with new life. Though none of those traditions is represented by itself in this book, all the authors note these changes and their profound effect, a lesson in the renewal of theological education that Dan has taught at every opportunity.

Donald Senior summarizes the gratitude of the authors and editor of this volume in a single sentence: "Few have reflected on the future of theological education with more insight, courage, and informed Christian wisdom than the man we honor with this volume." Fittingly, Dan's own reflections form the concluding chapter of this book.

PROMISES TO SERVE
Re-forming Lutheran Theological Education
David L. Tiede

INTRODUCTION: A TIME FOR TURNING

> *"After John had been arrested, Jesus went into Galilee. There he proclaimed the gospel from God saying, 'The time is fulfilled, and the kingdom of God is close at hand. Repent, and believe the gospel.'"*
> *(Mark 1:14–15, NJB)*

The year 2017 marked the five hundredth anniversary of Martin Luther's Ninety-Five Theses, publically posted in Wittenberg, Germany, on All Saints' Eve. Luther's first thesis echoed the call in the gospels of "Our Lord and Master Jesus Christ" for "the entire life of believers to be one of repentance."[1] In the sixteenth century, Luther was focused on the abuses of the church's disciplines of penance. But Jesus's first words in Mark's account speak to more than penance, resounding with profound biblical understandings of "turning toward God" (*metanoia*, Greek, or *shuv*, Hebrew). This is the Messiah's call to individuals and communities to the deep change of the mind and conversion of the heart that lead to lives of faith in the good news of God's reign in Christ Jesus.

This volume explores "Disruption and Hope" in twenty-first-century North American theological education. The theme requires our varied Christian traditions to deal practically with the demographic realities we are all facing in one form or another of ecclesiastical, social, and economic transitions. But the disruptions we face also mark a new God-given time for "turning," calling us to repent and believe in the good news of God's reign. And our varied Christian traditions have deep, distinctive wisdoms of discerning where God is at work in the whirlwinds of change.

It is a privilege to contribute this essay as a Lutheran voice in the conversation. The Lutheran seminaries accredited by the Association of Theological Schools (ATS) include two Concordia seminaries of the Lutheran Church–Canada (LC–C: 59,000 members in 301 congregations) in Edmonton, Alberta, and St. Catharines, Ontario, and two Concordia seminaries in the USA of the Lutheran Church–Missouri Synod (LCMS: 2,200,000 members in 6,200 congregations) in St. Louis, Missouri, and Fort Wayne, Indiana. The Evangelical Lutheran Church in Canada (ELCIC: 115,000 members in 525 congregations) has ATS-accredited seminaries in Waterloo, Ontario, and Saskatoon, Saskatchewan. And as of July 1, 2017, the Evangelical Lutheran Church in America (ELCA: 3,800,000 members in 10,000 congregations) has seven ATS-accredited seminaries in South Carolina, Pennsylvania, Ohio, Illinois, Iowa, Minnesota, and California.[2]

It is impossible to speak for all these Lutheran churches and their schools. Some seldom speak to each other. It is worth noting that all the seminaries have strong ecclesial identities, although financial support has diminished from all their church bodies. And they all are contending with enrollment challenges and anticipating clergy shortages amid decline in North American denominational memberships and worship attendance. The disruptions are real, but so are the legacies of faith. Merely grieving our losses and blaming others would be poor stewardship of the assets entrusted to us. We are not triumphal, but we believe God will prevail. To what repentance and hope are we Lutherans, among others, called in this time of turning?

This essay is an effort to prompt a sustained conversation among the Lutherans in the company of the ATS community of schools. Acknowledging the limitations of any one perspective in the maelstrom of change, I will first venture an interpretation of our distinctive Lutheran theological script of believing, belonging, and behaving, broadly shared among the many churches of the Lutheran World Federation, from Wittenberg onward ("I. Promises to Serve"). Then I will attempt a summary of some macrodisrupters that are converging commonly on North American education, including theological education ("II. Re-forming Theological Education"). I will conclude by focusing on the seven ELCA seminaries of my tradition and the profound regrouping of theological education we are now facing, pressing our 2017 "time for turning" to be more than institutional decompensation. To what faithful future is "our Lord and Master" calling us ("III. Called and Sent")?

I. PROMISES TO SERVE

Alasdair MacIntyre made the case for traditions of moral discourse in an age of relativism by describing a living tradition in ethics as a "historically extended, socially embodied argument, and an argument precisely in part about the goods which constitute that tradition." He also observed that "traditions, when vital, embody continuities of conflict," and he recognized the institution as "the bearer of a tradition of practice or practices."[3] MacIntyre's method illumines the social embodiments and confessional convictions of Christian traditions.

Every tradition of Christian theological education embodies convictions and practices to inform and form leadership for communities in their worship, witness, and service of God, the neighbor, and the world God loves. Justice churches and morality movements need distinctive kinds of education, as do Protestant missionary societies, Roman Catholic orders, and evangelistic communities of faith. The ATS is a singular context for traditions to learn from each other.

The several North American seminaries and schools that are heirs of the sixteenth-century Reformation have been disciplined in the study of the Christian Scriptures and attentive to their confessional identities. They have done excellent academic work, and they have developed distinctive approaches to the education of clergy, teachers, and community leaders for churches, institutions, and agencies who support and rely on them to do their work faithfully and well. Even as they serve increasingly ecumenical and interfaith groups, these theological seminaries are institutional embodiments of distinctive historic confessions or testimonies to God, Jesus Christ, the Holy Spirit, the church, and the world.[4]

What do the Lutherans bring to the ATS schools and their communities of witness and service? And how will Lutheran strengths be disciplined to serve the twenty-first-century callings of their own constituencies and to benefit broader ecumenical, interfaith, and international publics?

Lutherans have struggled among themselves, coming from varied European histories of orthodoxies, state churches and pietisms, coerced unions, and emigrations. In the early era of North American immigrations, the reality was that Lutheran communities needed pastors, "like sheep without a shepherd." Some were sent from the "mother churches" to ensure the Word of God would be "faithfully proclaimed" as Law and Gospel in the clarity of justification by grace through faith and the sacraments of baptism and the Lord's Supper would be "rightly administered." The immigrant groups brought Bibles, hymnals, and Luther's catechism in their own languages. Many also carried memories of painful conflicts with Roman Catholics, Reformed Protestants, and Pentecostals, exacerbated by the policies of the state churches.[5] As quickly as the Lutheran immigrants built houses of worship, their European-educated pastors founded training programs and seminaries in order that "the church might be planted" in the new land.[6]

By the time of the Civil War, the Lutherans were well established in eastern North America, but immigrations continued to flow into Lutheran communities until beyond World War II, especially throughout the western regions of the United States and Canada. The twenty-first-century landscape of North America continues to be unevenly spread with Lutheran "synods," some very small, others gathered into larger denominations, and all aspiring to be Christ's church.

The pastoral office has been held in high regard among Lutherans for serving God's people with the ministry of the Gospel and for being a ministry to the Gospel.[7] Just as Martin Luther continued to preach and administer the sacraments almost every week in the Wittenberg parish church, the faculties of North American Lutheran seminaries have been qualified for several generations by their pastoral and global mission experience as well as their academic credentials. The vocations of seminary professors and presidents continue to be honored as "teachers of the church," often speaking and writing on difficult issues,[8] providing leadership on ecumenical and interfaith consultations, and contributing educational resources for the churches.[9] Until recently, the presidents and chief executives of the Lutheran colleges and social ministry organizations were almost all ordained pastors. Lutherans have valued the theological knowledge and faith of their seminaries and their graduates. Leadership into a world of many cultures and religions is difficult yet promising when drawn from the wells of Lutheran theological wisdom.

The clarion declarations of the immigrant churches still resound true: "As goes the seminary, so goes the church!" "The seminary is where the future of the church is embodied." But what is the future into which God is calling the church, and how will the seminaries be turned to serve it?

The adjective "Lutheran" is both an asset and a liability. Martin Luther didn't like the idea of a church carrying his name. In the global world of Christian denominations, Lutherans regularly identify their church bodies as "Evangelical," which raises other questions. The Evangelical Lutheran Church in America, for example, must defend the integrity of its name against those who think it is an oxymoron because they don't regard Lutherans as evangelistic. But "Evangelical" is the crucial claim to define the identity of all the

Lutheran churches, not by their denominational boundaries, but by their center in the Gospel of Jesus Christ.

Lutherans' most vital watchword, therefore, is an evangelical declaration: "What serves Christ" (often quoted in German, *Was Christum treibet*). "What serves Christ" is as much a generative question as a declaration. This watchword reaches deeply into the scriptural assurance that the living Christ is at work in and through forgiven sinners and their imperfect institutions. This is not mere human optimism. This is the faith the missionary Bishop Lesslie Newbigin identified from the Apostle Paul (e.g., 2 Cor. 3:4, NRSV) as "proper confidence," because it is grounded in trust in "the fidelity of God."[10] This is also the theological conviction that gives Lutheran scriptural interpretation its heart for serving God's promises, in hermeneutical contrast to the ideals of scholasticism,[11] in tension with the Enlightenment's critical detachment, and in dismissal of all arrogance citing the Bible for national or ethnic superiority.

"What serves Christ" puts the church to work and calls upon Lutheran theological education to help communities of faith serve God's promises in Christ faithfully and effectively. Two of God's promises have framed a distinctive evangelical script to guide five centuries of Lutheran believing, belonging, and behaving for Christians and their communities. *Justification by grace through faith* and *Christian freedom to serve the neighbor* have been called the pillars of the Reformation, testifying both to God's love for undeserving mortals and to God's care for the world. Along with Christians of many other traditions, Lutherans are called to serve Christ by trusting in God's gracious promises in Christ Jesus to give ultimate worth to unworthy humans and to empower them to make the world trustworthy.

Justification by grace through faith, according to Martin Luther, is the teaching by which the church stands or falls. "God proves his love for us," declared Paul, "in that while we still were sinners Christ died for us." God does the "justifying," the "declaring or making righteous" of the ungodly, reconciling us through Christ even when at enmity with God (Rom. 3:21–26; 5:6–11). God's justification is the promise that defines the evangelical center for Lutheran identity and practice. This conviction requires disciplined theological leadership, frames Lutheran ecumenical and interfaith engagements, and empowers the missiology of this confessional tradition. There is nothing neutral or relativistic or generic in this core conviction. This is not a testimony that "God's in His heaven. All's right with the world." Israel's law, prophets, and writings bear witness along with the Christian gospels, letters, and writings to the compassion of God in the midst of the broken human condition and the travail of the creation itself. And God's love in Christ Jesus will prevail. As Paul, Augustine, Luther, Reinhold Niebuhr, and Dietrich Bonhoeffer (among others) saw, all humans, families, communities, and societies are ultimately unable to save themselves. In Christ, God acted from outside of us (extra nos) to rescue us personally and socially from being turned in on our self-righteousness (curvatus in se).[12]

Grounded in the "theology of the cross,"[13] God's compassion is disclosed in the human horrors of Jesus's crucifixion and the carnage of war. "Justification by grace through faith" cuts sharply into all opportunistic forms of self-justification. Trusting God's love even for the alienated and ungodly rejects the culture's doctrinaire optimism in human progress and self-fulfillment.[14] This faith corrects and heals the triumphal arrogance of nationalistic religion. God's commands and promises both reveal our compromised mortal plight and welcome us to life in Christ.[15]

To serve its evangelical confession, Lutheran theological education must turn and return, again and anew, to "What serves Christ" in the faith of people, communities, and institutions. Alert to the issues and problems confronting communities of faith and informed by ecumenical Biblical, theological, ethical, historical, and ministerial scholarship, the vocation of Lutheran theological education means repentance and faith in the God who justifies the ungodly in Christ Jesus.

This is also the Lutheran calling in interchurch and interfaith relationships. "Justification by grace through faith" has provided the biblical/confessional standard for ecumenism, adjudicating dogmatic

19

divisions among the Christian churches of European origin and yearning for full communion throughout the Body of Christ. The authenticity of interfaith engagements is strengthened when the voice of each faith speaks from the soul of its beliefs and practices. Seeking to understand one another's faith is crucial, especially among Muslims, Jews, and Christians. Jesus of Nazareth holds fascination for all faiths, and no one can surpass his welcome of everyone. Thus serving God's radical promise of justification in Christ Jesus empowers our gracious engagement with our neighbor's faith.

The sixteenth-century Reformation sought to "Christianize Christendom"[16] in a culture where almost everyone was baptized and there was little social or theological understanding of either Jews or Muslims as people of faith. That awareness dawned slowly in subsequent centuries as world mission movements encountered new lands and religions. From the pietists to the orthodox confessionalists, the North American Lutherans supported international missions and encouraged evangelistic practices in their communities, often learning, albeit slowly, from their returning missionaries. When the missionaries stayed centered in God's love for the world in Christ Jesus, they could see that God had been at work in other cultures long before Western Christians showed up. Substantial work continues to be done among Lutherans to ground their apostolic missions in God's promise of "justification by grace through faith" to the world, including those once thought to be outsiders. To quote Robert Bertram, "*Promissio* is the secret of *missio*."[17]

And the missionary era taught the Lutherans to understand the lesson the apostles gave to "the entire house of Israel" that "the promise is for you, and for your children, and for all who are far away, everyone whom the Lord our God calls to him" (Acts 2:36–39). Israel did not possess the promise for itself but was called to serve God's global intent. After five centuries of living within and extending Christendom, Lutherans are being called to "turn" to serve God's mission.

More than a pillar of the Reformation to be restored, justification in the full scriptural narrative is God's promise to bless the

20

neighbor, near and far, and the world itself. In the Acts of the Apostles (1:6–8), Jesus's last words on earth echo God's word to Israel through Isaiah (49:6), enlarging the church's vision beyond restoration of a treasured past to bearing God's light to the ends of the earth. To serve God's promise of justification, the church itself in every generation must turn from preoccupation with preservation to hearing and enacting God's commission.

Christian freedom to serve the neighbor may be called the second pillar of the Reformation, and this freedom is again empowered by God's promise as a dynamic complement to justification by grace through faith. In his 1520 treatise on "The Freedom of a Christian," Martin Luther echoed the Apostle Paul (1 Cor. 9:19), declaring,

A Christian is lord of all, completely free of everything.
A Christian is a servant, completely attentive to the needs of all.[18]

This freedom/vocation is stirred from within the compassion of God's justification, which we did not deserve. Every effort to prove our worth before God reveals lack of faith in what God has done for us in Christ Jesus. Our "good works" earn us no merit with God, as if we could bring a claim of righteousness before God, even by our obedience to God's commands. Confident in God's liberation, we are called into God's mission of love for the world as forgiven sinners. This vocation is a pillar of the Reformation that is personally and socially empowering.

Our vocation to care for our neighbor and the world is holy because Christ, who loves our neighbor and the world, is living in us. Living in dependence on God's promises in Christ, we are freed to do actual, practical good for our neighbors and the world God loves, without always needing to get it right. God has given our human efforts a proper place in the economy of the risen Christ, a practical role in serving our neighbors and the world God loves. The risen Christ empowers my life and our life together.[19]

Christians are called to serve God's promise of Christian freedom as robustly as we have treasured God's promise of justification. "What serves Christ" is trust in what God's love has done for us (freedom from . . . see Rom. 5:8), and this faith is active in love for others (freedom for . . . see Gal. 5:6). Martin Luther's teaching of Christian freedom protested against sixteenth-century religious suppression. God's promise of freedom in Christ now contends with commodified messages of freedom that have no need of God and secularized schemes of success and self-fulfillment. The freedom that "serves Christ" by loving the neighbor liberates the soul without manipulation.

The conviction of Christian freedom also interacts with a broad range of "liberation" movements dealing with economic, social, and political realities as well as racial and gender identities. The narratives in the Acts of the Apostles about God's care for people of varied abilities, gender identities, and social locations are often more radically helpful in many liberation contexts than Luther's affirmations of freedom. He was, after all, a sixteenth-century Saxon.

In the present time of repentance and renewal, Lutherans have work to do to serve God's promise of Christian freedom with the many significant strengths already entrusted to them. These include the vocations of all the baptized to make the world more trustworthy for their families, communities, work, and public life; the capacities of Lutheran educational systems to equip their graduates for lifelong callings; and the ministries of mercy and justice of local and global Lutheran and other social service agencies.

In an era of denominational decline, the Lutherans in North America (as tallied earlier in this essay) include millions of members in thousands of worshipping congregations, plus hundreds of camps and retreat centers and regional or synodical organizations with national and international assemblies. But these are only the metrics of church organizations. God's empowerment of the baptized, however, is fundamentally a promise to the neighbor and the world.

At least since 1991, when Loren Mead published *The Once and Future Church*,[20] many North American denominations have accepted his proposal that the church's mission frontier now lies at the doorstep of the worshipping community. This consensus has prompted a broad diversity of ways for the churches to be in mission, displaying the theological convictions of each tradition and prompting differing expectations of the leadership needed for mission.

Lutheran worship is focused on serving God's promise of justification, the ultimate consolation of the love of Christ for this life and the next. Well known for their singing,[21] the Lutherans are now learning to praise God in many musical vernaculars. Although the liturgy regularly concludes with the commission "Go in peace, serve the Lord," the weekly "gathering" is less consistently turned outside of itself to honor the commission of the people. The "sending" of the faithful, as those whom Martin Luther called "little Christs," to the neighbor and the world is an enactment of the promise of Christian freedom. The mission consequence of this practice would be to follow up the next Sunday with the question "How did it go last week?" "What serves Christ" is the vocation of millions of forgiven sinners, empowered to bear the mercy and justice of Christ to their neighbors and the world. And how can we best care for the neighbors God has given to us in the twenty-first century, where every worshipping community is virtually connected with "those who are far away, everyone whom the Lord our God calls to him" (Acts 2:39, NRSV) and increasingly surrounded by a diversity that Christendom never envisioned?

The promise of Christian freedom has long been experienced by many as blessing their lives with courage and conviction in the midst of the joys and the sorrows of family, work, public life, and the community of faith. Among other Christians, therefore, the Lutherans who live by their faith in God's promises are called to the repentance of turning the church outside in and inside out for the sake of the neighbor and the world God so loves.

From the time of the community chest in Wittenberg, Lutherans formed alliances with all kinds of groups seeking the best wisdom of what will actually serve human need. The relative success of northern European socialism in the state churches may be credited, in part, to this practicality. Lutherans respect the public realm as the arena where God's second promise of Christian freedom empowers engagement with all people of goodwill, Christian or not. The immigrant North American Lutherans lavishly invented institutions in health care, social service, and education beyond what the numbers of Lutherans required for their own needs. Lutheran hospitals now have largely been absorbed in larger health care systems, but vital Lutheran social services and education continue at an impressive scale. This Lutheran institutional strategy enjoys enduring support from broad publics, usually across the political spectrum.

Some Lutheran institutions even explicitly claim the script of God's promises as they build public partnerships with state, national, and international funding sources. The website of Lutheran Social Service of Minnesota (LSS-MN; lssmn.org), for example, announces that it "expresses the love of Christ for all people through service that inspires hope, changes lives, and builds community."

The mission of LSS-MN is "grounded in two principles—*God loves all people without condition and God yearns for us to love the neighbor.*" Those two "principles" articulate the Lutheran understanding of God's promises, and the agency advocates for those in need. The vast majority of LSS-MN's $121,792,445 for 2015 budget came from state support, from both sides of the legislative aisle. Other national and international examples can also be identified.[22]

Through their tensions with each other, the LCMS and the Evangelical Lutheran Church in America (ELCA) have sustained their collaborations in social services while also hosting their own aid initiatives. In these human care engagements, both the ELCA and the LCMS have gathered public and private partnerships and networked with congregations and local agencies to build facilities for the elderly, the disabled, and the homeless (notably adolescents) and to support adoptions and refugee resettlement without requirements of Lutheran affiliation from clients or most staff. Lutherans try to be vigilant to honor God's promised justification through Christ, and they are freed by God's second promise to work with all people of goodwill to help the neighbor in need.

This distinctive bifocal strategy requires institutional leadership in a world of many cultures, religions, and secularization. While their economic scale is much greater than the support they receive from Lutheran denominational budgets, all these agencies maintain close ties with their churches, nurture constituencies of support among congregations and their members, and host opportunities to learn from their theological heritage. Lutheran Services of America, for example, regularly welcomes a "theologian in residence" in its board meetings,[23] and LSS-MN has drawn upon college and seminary faculty to provide a course of study for congregations to sustain their commitments to relate positively to Muslim immigrants.[24]

Education has long been an asset for Lutherans to serve God's promise of Christian freedom. Schools of every level, emphatically including education for girls, were an immediate enterprise for Martin Luther and Philip Melanchthon, extending through building the faculty and curricula for the University of Wittenberg. Lutheran immigrants to North America promptly established schools, primarily by supporting public education while providing pastoral leadership for religious instruction in congregations and homes.

The LCMS built a robust private "system" with primary and secondary schools, junior colleges, senior colleges, and seminaries. The LCMS Concordia University System now includes ten colleges and universities in the US, networked with the educational institutions of the Lutheran Church–Canada and other global partners.

The ELCA currently has a roster of twenty-six colleges and universities. Almost all these higher education institutions were founded to serve students from Lutheran families and congregations to prepare the next generation of pastors, teachers, medical doctors and nurses, and other professionals. Their presidents were usually ordained clergy, and their faculties were often Lutherans with research degrees from North American or European universities.

In the post–World War II decades, these Lutheran colleges strengthened in academic quality and enrolled increasingly diverse student bodies and faculties at the same time that direct financial support from their church bodies decreased in their budgets. For a few, Lutheran identity belongs to the past. Some of their faculties wondered if the word "Lutheran" should be dropped. Could the case for Lutheran higher education be more than denominational dollars and students?

Other presidents, faculty, staff, students, board members, graduates, church leaders, and constituents have joined the search for renewed understandings and evidence of the distinctive value of Lutheran higher education. As has already been observed, Lutherans understand God's promise of Christian freedom practically. This tradition in higher education is not a disembodied idea, but it is, in Alasdair MacIntyre's term, "socially embodied" and entrusted to Lutherans.

Well before the current "disruptions" caused all institutions of higher education to demonstrate the value of their distinctive brand promise,[25] an amazing range of essays, presentations, and books had been produced on the case for Lutheran higher education.[26] How the institutions of higher education work together is important in itself. But more than institutional competence is needed. In *The Gift and Task of Lutheran Higher Education*, for example, Tom Christenson also explored "the way a faith tradition might shape our understanding of the educational task."[27]

Three examples of how its faith tradition and institutional history are shaping Lutheran higher education can be highlighted as a context for the re-forming of ELCA seminaries in particular.

1. In the 1990s, the ELCA seminaries convened three "clusters" of the ELCA colleges and social ministries in the west (the Western Mission Cluster), midwest (the Covenant Cluster), and the east (the Eastern Cluster) to explore their shared responsibilities for educating leaders for the church. Tracking with the ELCA's 1995 Study of Theological Education, the discussion veered between defending the number and location of existing seminaries to advancing proposals on how to prepare the leaders needed for the future in more places. The faith question of what is needed from these leaders for the communities to "serve Christ" informed the exploration of how to configure the educational task.

2. The quest to discern the vocation of a Lutheran college has been advanced by ongoing consultations of the colleges and

supported by denominational leadership, even as church funding for the schools' budgets diminished. In 2007, the ELCA adopted a social statement on "Our Calling in Education" (https://www.elca .org/Faith/Faith-and-Society/Social-Statements/Education). The statement announced, "Education belongs to our baptismal vocation. Our particular calling in education is two-fold: to educate people in the Christian faith for their vocation and to strive with other to ensure that all have access to high-quality education that develops person gifts and abilities and serves the common good. This calling embraces all people in both Church and society." The ELCA colleges and universities are not always of one mind on how their Lutheran identity may be educationally and institutionally promising. But their council of presidents has welcomed Professor Darrell Jodock's presentation on "The Third Path, Religious Diversity, and Civil Discourse." Jodock demonstrates that God's promise of Christian freedom sets Lutheran education apart from the either "secular" or "sectarian" private colleges and universities. He documents how non-Christians can benefit from a Lutheran college's rootedness in Christian freedom "because precisely this rootedness has secured a place for the non-Christian's full participation in the community."[28]

3. Prompted by Lilly Endowment's grants for "The Theological Exploration of Vocation," several ELCA colleges and universities, including many that did not receive a grant, have encouraged faculty, students, and graduates to renew and mobilize the Lutheran tradition's commitments to education for lives of purpose and service. At the most practical level, these colleges and universities are engaging more students in how they will find "meaningful work"[29] in the world. Students of every religious or nonreligious identity benefit through richer understandings of purposeful living, and their parents approve of their increased prospects for employment. But this "theological exploration" also leads deeper into Lutheran convictions that what makes work truly "meaningful" is the gift of God's calling or vocation. For those who can receive it, this is a recognition of God's promise of Christian freedom, freedom from needing to prove ourselves and freedom for blessing the neighbor and the world. And

for those who can receive that freedom as God's promise, this is faith in God's deep promise of justification by grace.

II. Re-forming Theological Education

As noted earlier, this essay welcomes the turning (*metanoia*) of the ELCA theological seminaries without presuming to address the changes needed by other Christian traditions in the United States and Canada. But as the range of essays in this volume discloses, *Disruption and Hope* may well be the narrative of almost all current North American theological education.

Thirty years ago, a seasoned pastor wrote a letter to a newly elected seminary president with a message that has been quoted as prophetic throughout the ATS: "Quit preparing your graduates for a church that no longer exists." Although their church identities varied significantly, the challenge rang true across the range of mainline, evangelical, Episcopal, Lutheran, and Roman Catholic schools because their ministers, pastors, priests, and church leaders were reporting a profoundly changed context for their ministries. Then the questions became systemic. For what future church should the seminaries prepare their graduates? And how would the seminaries need to change and be changed to do this work faithfully, effectively, and efficiently?

In the next twenty years, many ATS seminaries labored to improve. They collaborated with national church leaders to "cluster" and "network" with each other and vital congregations, colleges, universities, social ministries, retreat centers and camps, and continuing education programs. They also built constituencies of financial support and assumed increasingly strong roles in student recruitment, and they reframed and reformed their curricular strategies. New initiatives included interfaith engagements, programs in Islamic studies, and explorations of how congregations can be equipped to empower the vocations of all the baptized in the world. Instead of focusing on regulating the schools, denominational officers often collaborated with the seminaries to help them build boards and constituencies that would strengthen their capacities.

Many seminaries had once been primarily "abbeys," kept by the churches to nurture leaders in the faith in "seedbeds" of theological formation. Then they became "academies," taking their places among the intellectually best schools in North America and Europe. Now they were called to be "apostolates," to send forth the leaders Christian and other communities of faith need for a new era of service in a changing world. Seminary faculties and administrators were hoping to improve in all three modes, some more radically as an abbey, an academy, or an apostolate. Daniel Aleshire, the executive director of the ATS, encouraged the schools to "learn to be apostolates, providing the intellectual and educational support that the Christian project will require as it moves into a new era in North America and blossoms with new energy elsewhere in the world."[30]

The decade that began in 2007 was another story. Thomas L. Friedman introduces the first major chapter of his recent book *Thank You for Being Late* with a fierce question that is quasi-theological: "What the Hell Happened in 2007?"[31] In this collection of ATS essays, we might prefer to ask, "What in Heaven's Name Happened in 2007?" In either theological frame, the question signals a profound change. Where is God in the disruptions?

The past decade demonstrates how deeply the small universe of North American theological education has been disrupted. Theological schools, moreover, are connected, explicitly or indirectly, to their benefit or peril, with churches and other communities of faith and religious practice. It may be helpful to name four "disrupters" that no school chose and that are converging on all ATS institutions. How will the schools, including the Lutherans, respond faithfully and effectively?

1. The digitization and marketing of everything are transforming higher education profoundly, and these twin forces pervade the world of theological learning and teaching. The marketing of diverse programs has opened traditional curricula of ordination studies, requiring financial plans to demonstrate their market viability. Without identifying even a portion of the alterations in the educational practices of ATS schools, the cybernetic revolution with its business metrics has transformed theological education more than the printing press in the sixteenth-century Reformation. There is no way back to a predigital era.

2. The cost/debt spiral is commonly identified as a game-changer in higher education, notably through its impact on enrollments. The effect has been compounded in the economies of ATS schools by the persistent decline in denominational finances. Only a few schools are adequately funded by church or endowment support. Managing expenses continues to be a necessary, but not sufficient, discipline for sustaining the seminaries' educational missions. Growing revenues requires rallying committed constituencies.

3. The need for leadership education in change challenges historic understandings of pastoral care for stable communities of faith. The ATS standards for curricula still call broadly for the development of "an aptitude for theological reflection and wisdom pertaining to responsible life in faith."[32] But in a time when both seminaries and the communities they serve are facing disruptive changes, their leadership must be adaptive, innovative, and courageous.

4. The focus on educational results gives new accountability to theological education. Each of the first three "disrupters" both threatens the way schools have operated and proposes pathways forward. The focus on "outcomes" came through the ATS's governmental authorization to accredit schools, and it first felt like an insult, until the ATS and the member schools claimed its promise. As with the digitization of learning, the metrics of quality are now primarily the measurements of what the students learned, not the strength of the school's faculty and teaching resources. The pressure for change continues to come from outside.

III. CALLED AND SENT

This essay is being written in the five hundredth anniversary year of the Protestant Reformation. As noted above, this third section of the essay will focus on the seven ELCA seminaries of my tradition and their profound regrouping of theological education, pressing our 2017 "time for turning" to be more than institutional decompensation.

The situation of the ELCA seminaries is sobering. Some will say the system is imploding, and the critics may blame the tragic blindness of presidents, boards, and church leaders for not recognizing how profoundly the world was changing as institutional destabilization accelerated. Analysts may be tempted to predict the situation will only grow worse, and they may be right, especially if their gloomy prognostications become the dominant message. But even in the worst of times, the Lord's call to turn is grounded in a narrative of faith.

The turning has already begun amid the disruptions of the ELCA seminaries. Curriculum reforms—focused effective leadership of Christian communities, programs engaged with social needs, increased collaborations with church bodies, and notably, organizational mergers between seminaries in one case and with other Lutheran educational institutions in three others are completed or under way.[33]

The turning, the *metanoia*, to which the ELCA seminaries are being called, is about more than institutional preservation. The relief the embedded seminaries feel at being "bailed out" will be brief. The wisdom of the Lutheran universities that have merged, yoked, or collaborated with these seminaries may be questioned if the seminaries' resources (faculties, properties, and financial assets) are the only prize. In the larger disrupted world of higher education, some embedded seminaries in other traditions have already become financial and educational headaches for their host schools.

Even serving as merged ELCA institutions requires a deeper conviction than Lutheran loyalty. Privileged attention is owed to the communities of Christian worship and service who rely on the theological schools to do their work well, as they call pastors, teachers, and leaders to serve among them. As the supply diminishes, a thousand ELCA congregations who could afford to call a pastor are already unable to find one. And what of the larger Body of Christ bearing God's care for the billions of people in the world of many cultures and religions and for the earth itself?

"What serves Christ," therefore, is finally the only rationale for saving the seminaries, and the authentic case for Lutheran theological education is to serve God's promises of justification by grace through faith and Christian freedom in a new time. How does the current destabilization of "what has been" in this small universe of seminaries provide new opportunities for moving beyond restoration of the past into God's mission of mercy and justice to the ends of the earth?

Addressing the disruptors identified above, to what "turn" (*metanoia/shuv*) is "our Lord and Master" calling and sending the ELCA's seminaries and what are their assets in this turning?

1. The digitization and marketing of everything are accelerating all the disruptions. They are as pervasive, unremitting, and unforgiving in the world of theological education as everywhere else. The Lutherans put on a brave face early in this turbulence, recalling how deftly Martin Luther adopted the printing press.[34] Challenging as it is to keep focused on "What serves Christ," the Lutherans are seeking to learn practical lessons:

> a. Lesson one is that "distance learning" misses a point that "distributed learning" catches. Instead of perpetuating the seminary's role as teaching center to supply knowledge, concentrated and broadcast from faculties, libraries, and campuses, the motive center is located where learning cohorts gather, off and on campus. Formation of leaders requires localized communities of learning, informed by conversations with colleagues and worship. This "outside-in" paradigm shift is not yet complete. But to equip leadership for a distributed network of Christian communities, the digital technologies must become toolkits for effective learning communities so the seminaries can reconfigure their campus centers intelligently.

b. Lesson two is that emerging generations of learners are natives in the digital world. And if the cybercontext is native for the seminarians, it is even more profoundly real for those still younger and their families and their communities. Entering the media cultures of coming generations will be as challenging and important as "translating the message" has been in cross-cultural missions.[35]

c. Lesson three is that the age of accelerations creates a renewed role for communities, and particularly communities of faith, in sustaining humanity and the creation. This is Tom Friedman's concluding appreciation for his Jewish community of origin, as expressed in the title *Thank You for Being Late*.[36] In the "age of accelerations," the vocation of Christian communities is being renewed.

2. The cost/debt spiral has disrupted theological schools profoundly. Rising student debt of those entering seminary has been compounded by increased tuitions in institutions whose revenue sources have declined. These schools have also welcomed increasing numbers of "second career," racial-ethnic, ecumenical, and international students, many with complex financial profiles. In the stressed economies of theological seminaries, administrations, faculty, students, constituencies, and boards have struggled to accomplish their school's educational mission while sustaining its financial viability.

The ELCA schools are a dramatic demonstration of moving from being subsidized by the denomination to building funding programs that rely on people with a heart for the future of the church and its pastors. These schools have all had to make deep program cuts and achieve institutional savings in quest of sustainable economies. Financial disruptions will continue to require astute and courageous leadership. Significant lessons are being learned:

a. The students are already benefitting from a financial mentoring program that an ELCA seminary designed with support from a donor, and this model has been widely shared. Experienced lay leaders are first paired with students to help them develop a realistic financial plan for getting through seminary with minimal debt. Their intern supervisors then introduce them to faithful people in the congregation to learn how these generous people became good stewards and why they give. In their first calls, perhaps after an annual meeting or two, they are then ready to benefit from workshops on building stewardship programs in their congregations.

b. While the faculties of ELCA seminaries have experienced the pain of faltering economies, they are also learning the financial disciplines of building the donor bases and modifying their curricula to accomplish better results at less cost.

c. As the ELCA's national organization and supporting synods have experienced significant declines in financial support, they have sought to keep seminary funding as a priority. They have also learned to encourage the development efforts of the schools and taken the initiative in building an endowed Fund for Leaders, supporting students at ELCA seminaries.

d. The administrations and boards have made remarkable strides in learning to practice "governance as leadership" in its fiduciary, strategic, and generative dimensions.[37] Boards have become more astute at cost management, and they are learning to take leadership in developing their school's revenues.

3. The need for leadership in change may be as difficult for the communities of faith as for their schools. Both are known for treasuring their established ways. Transforming theological education to become leadership education disrupts "the way we used to do it," when our excellence was measured by our mastery of the fields of study. The move toward leadership education is seen by some as an intellectual insult, since teaching "theory" and "the assured results of scholarship" have long been held in higher academic regard than "application in practice." But instead of "dumbing down" the classic teaching of theological education, this turn is a renewal of learning, a return to learning what the Spirit is teaching in communities of faith and the lives of Christians in the world.

For decades, well-meaning people have compiled impossibly long lists of "practical courses you should teach at the seminary"— for example, running a business, planning, evangelism, advocacy for justice, more training in counseling, and required classes in steward-ship, youth ministry, care for the elderly, and so on. But the more forceful impetus for a turn toward leadership education came first from outside the seminaries, from thoughtful pastors and laity in congregations, social ministries, and continuing education centers. They had something deeper in mind. They spoke with passion and concern: "You need to know what we are confronting!" Their voices were both loyal and critical. They saw that changes the schools need to make are profound and systemic, because the Evangelical com-munities of faith they serve are confronting disruptive challenges to their fidelity and viability.

The curricular reforms of the ELCA seminaries in the past decades display their efforts to draw wisely from the deep wells of the established academic theological disciplines. In educating, form-ing, and equipping seminarians for leadership of changing Christian communities who trust in God's promises, the ELCA seminaries are now also learning from the broader disciplines of leadership educa-tion in higher education and business. These newer educational fields are increasingly seeded with social and anthropological studies. The seminaries' curricular designs are being re-formed to sustain teach-ing of the Lutheran Evangelical confession in new contexts while also learning to "read the audiences"—that is, exploring how to serve God's promises within dynamic family and congregation systems, public community economics, and the accelerations of change.

This work is all fully practical and deeply theological, as it must be for Lutherans. In the sixteenth-century debates about Christ's presence in the sacraments, Luther and his followers, grounded in the scriptural story of promise, resisted metaphysical speculations. As the Word made flesh reveals, God loves the finite, physical, and historical world. By God's mercy, the created world is capable of bearing the infinite, spiritual, and eternal. The incarnation narrative informs the evangelical, world-affirming wisdom of this tradition.

4. The focus on educational results is altering the hegemony of established academic disciplines in all higher education. This change of mind, however, may hold more promise than threat for theological education. The ELCA's schools in particular are closely bonded with those who depend on them to do their work well. The proposal of this essay is that "What serves Christ" puts Lutheran theological education to work attending to the evangelical script of God's promises of justification and Christian freedom. If that is even close to right, discerning the "results" communities of faith and service need now from their leaders continues to be complex, inspiring, and empowering, if difficult to measure!

This "turning" is happening. On reading the websites of the ELCA seminaries and in conferring with knowledgeable observers, one can observe the change of mind in their institutional repositioning, curricular strategies, and leadership successions. Their attention to results enhances the ability of these schools to meet accreditation standards and much more. These "turns" are forays by seven schools into the future of the church, conducted without guarantees of success, seeking to learn and provide the leadership communities of faith most need. The learning curve is steep, but this intellectual and spiritual "turning" is a quest to serve the promises of Christ. The identities of each of these schools differ, and their institutional futures are in play, but they also share profound theological and institutional assets, none of which is uniquely Lutheran, but all distinctively so. They are seeking to master crucial lessons:

a. The ELCA seminaries are all centered in the script of "What serves Christ."

b. They are all embedded in the network of congregations, social ministries, and institutions of higher education that are already engaged ecumenically, socially, cross-culturally, and interreligiously in God's mercy and justice for the neighbor and the world. These initiatives are exercises in Christian freedom, stirring the hearts of younger generations. The global distribution of Lutheran seminary graduates from many decades is remarkable, such as the rapidly growing Mekane Yesus Evangelical Church in Ethiopia, now the largest member of the Lutheran World Federation.

c. The ELCA seminaries are being re-formed to prepare leaders for Christian communities in a dynamic, pluralistic, postdenominational world.

CONCLUSION: SERVING THE PROMISES

Five centuries ago, Martin Luther echoed the call in the gospels of "Our Lord and Master Jesus Christ for the entire life of believers to be one of repentance."[38] The disrupted church was re-formed by the Lord's call to "repent and believe the gospel." This call to faith was grounded in the promise "The time is fulfilled, and the kingdom of God is close at hand" (Mark 1:15).

The present era of accelerated change is again a time of repentance, of metanoia, of turning. The churches and their seminaries are being turned inside out by disruptions of historic strengths and outside in by the Spirit. This is not a re-formation the institutions chose. The temptations to blame or despair are real. But our Lord's declaration continues to be "Repent and believe in the gospel." The hopeful way forward is by faith in God's promises.[39]

God's love for the world extends through the progress and pathos of human history. The Lutheran evangelical confession affirms God's creation and embodies a local and global calling. In a world that is often lonely and unforgiving, thousands of Christian communities and millions of people rely on the seminaries to equip the leadership they need to serve God's promises of justification by grace through faith and Christian freedom to serve the neighbor and the world.

The five hundredth anniversary of the Ninety-Five Theses is a challenging and promising time for Lutheran theological education.

2

FROM CANTERBURY TO CAPETOWN
Perspectives on Anglican Theological Education
Martha J. Horne

Theological education in the Anglican Communion has traditionally placed equal emphasis on the importance of the life of the mind in Christian faith and the importance of individual and communal formation for ministry. These dual commitments, combined with a commitment to a learned clergy, provided the framework on which curricula were developed for Episcopal seminaries in the United States, beginning with the establishment of the General Theological Seminary in New York in 1817 and the Protestant Episcopal Theological Seminary in Virginia in 1823.[1] A close look at those and later Episcopal seminaries in the United States reveals a consistent pattern in which rigorous academic study of Scripture and the classical theological disciplines occurs alongside the development of pastoral and practical ministerial skills and the cultivation of spiritual disciplines and practices necessary for a life of faithful and productive ministry.

Until recently, there was a consensus among Anglicans that theological education and preparation for ordained ministry should take place in a residential setting where worship, study, prayer, and fellowship are integrated into a rhythm of life that is itself formative.

It was a model of formation that replicated the rhythms and practices of monastic communities.

In recent years, changes within the church and the religious land-scape of North America have made it necessary to develop new models for theological education. Theological education is no longer understood as being primarily for those who are seeking ordination but is now recognized as important in the formation of laity as well as clergy. Because fewer seminaries can sustain an educational model based on full-time residential programs, new models are being devel-oped and implemented. The rapid pace of change within the church and American culture makes it increasingly important to identify the essential components of an Anglican approach to theological educa-tion so that they can be preserved and integrated into new models.

As other essays in this volume will confirm, Anglican seminar-ies in the United States and Canada share many of the same commit-ments and experience many of the same challenges as our colleagues in theological schools of other denominations represented within the Association of Theological Schools (ATS). Since many of the current challenges are related to changes in the religious landscape of North America, a brief review of some of these changes will provide a con-text for what follows.

I. The Changing Landscape

Signs of the decline of religion in American are reported regularly by researchers who gather data through interviews, surveys, and polls. Recent data reveal a steady decline in church attendance and self-reported religious affiliation among Americans. These trends have a direct impact on theological schools. In March of 2015, the Gen-eral Social Survey (GSS) released data from its 2014 survey.[2] For forty-two years, the GSS has asked about religious preferences: "Is it Protestant, Catholic, Jewish, some other religion, or no religion? The percentage answering 'no religion' (the 'nones') was 21 per cent in 2014, but only 8 percent in 1990, meaning that the percentage of Americans with no religious preference increased 13 percentage points in 24 years."[3] Noting that each percentage point represents 2.5 million adults, Tobin Grant cited these data in a 2015 Religion News Service blog with the headline "ANALYSIS: 7.5 Million Lost Their Religion Since 2012."[4] It should be noted that the 2014 GSS also reports that "preferring no religion is not atheism, which is still very rare. In 2014, just 3 percent of Americans said that they did not believe in God."[5]

Religion among Millennials

The millennial generation, now between the ages of nineteen to thirty-six, is the largest generational cohort in the United States and the largest generation in the work force. In 2016 the *Atlantic* introduced a special project on religious disaffiliation and choice among American millennials under the heading "How Will Young People Choose Their Religion?" Among its findings are data confirming that "people in their 20s and early 30s account for more than a third of the country's 'nones.'"[6] A Religious Landscape Study conducted by Pew Research Center in 2014 reported that only 27 percent of millennials attend religious services weekly, considerably fewer than 38 percent of baby boomers and 51 percent of the silent and greatest generations, born before 1945.

These statistics cause many to wonder about the future of religion in America, the role of the church in American society, and the future of theological schools created to serve the mission and ministries of the church. The statistics are important, but more information is required to provide a clearer picture of the current landscape. As the *Atlantic* article observes, "If young people don't care about religion, the thinking goes, that necessarily means the United States will become a much less religious country over time . . . but while church attendance may be down, that doesn't say much about people finding church outside the walls of a sanctuary."[7] Similarly, although millennials are less affiliated with a particular denomination or faith, Pew Research Center data confirm that "they are as likely to engage in many spiritual practices. Like older Americans, more than four-in-ten of these younger adults say they feel a deep sense of wonder about the universe at least once a week, 55% say they think about the meaning and purpose of life on a weekly basis, and 51% say they feel a deep sense of spiritual peace and well-being at least once a week."[8]

Episcopal Church Data

Research data from the Episcopal Church reveal significant declines in the number of baptized members over the past ten years, coupled with a decline in average Sunday church attendance (ASA). Seventy-one percent of congregations had an ASA of one hundred or fewer in 2015, while only 4 percent had an ASA of three hundred or more. Fifty-nine percent of Episcopal congregations in the United States are in villages or small towns, many of which are also experiencing a decline in population. Most small churches within the denomination are becoming smaller, and while some large churches are growing, especially in urban and suburban areas, the number of congregations with more than five hundred members has declined.[9]

With fewer members and declining average Sunday attendance, an increasing number of congregations can no longer afford the cost of a full-time stipendiary priest. As a result, the number of ordinations to the priesthood in the Episcopal Church has declined sharply, and the number of part-time and bivocational clergy continues to grow. Many candidates for ordination are reluctant to leave jobs and move families for three years of full-time residential study with no certainty that a full-time paid position will be available when they graduate.

Episcopal seminaries in the United States are experiencing the cumulative effects of all these factors, which contribute to a "perfect storm": declining enrollments; congregations that are shrinking in size and in the capacity to pay clergy, maintain buildings, or support theological schools; fewer people claiming any religious affiliation; the changing role of Christianity in North America; and a growing climate of anti-intellectualism in the United States. All these forces threaten the financial sustainability and survival of theological schools.

What does this crisis mean for the future of theological education for Anglicans in the United States and Canada? How do we address current realities while also planning for a future that we know will be different but whose shape is still uncertain? For all the unknowns, one thing is clear: the future cannot and will not look like the past. Too much has changed and too much is at stake not to acknowledge current realities. Given all the uncertainties, what are the implications for an Anglican approach to theological education? What values, traditions, and practices from a long and rich heritage are resources for the future of Anglican theological education?

II. THE "ANGLICAN WAY"

In 2001 the Primates of the Anglican Communion determined that a working party on theological education should be established as an expression of their strong commitment to theological education throughout the worldwide Communion. Theological Education for the Anglican Communion (TEAC) was created and began its work the following year. In 2007 TEAC issued a statement titled "The Anglican Way: Signposts on a Common Journey," the culmination of a four-year process in which church leaders, theologians, and educators gathered from around the world to discuss the teaching of Anglican identity, life, and practice. The "Signpost" statement was intended to form the basis for how Anglicanism is taught at all levels of learning for laity, clergy, and bishops.[10] It describes "the Anglican Way" as "a particular expression of the Christian Way of being the One, Holy, Catholic, and Apostolic Church of Jesus Christ: formed by Scripture, shaped through worship, ordered for communion, and directed by God's mission."[11]

Scripture, communion, worship, and mission: each of these has implications for the other three, and all four are central to an Anglican understanding of theological education. What follows are observations and reflections on the ways in which each has traditionally shaped the curriculum of theological education within Anglican institutions and how they can contribute to a vision for the future.

III. SCRIPTURE AS THE PRIMARY SOURCE OF AUTHORITY FOR ANGLICANS

TEAC adopted Ephesians 4:12–13 as its foundational scriptural text: "To equip the saints for the work of ministry, for building up the body of Christ, until all of us come to the unity of the faith and of the knowledge of the Son of God, to maturity, to the measure of the full stature of Christ."

In making Scripture the starting point for its work, TEAC affirmed the primacy of Scripture among the traditional sources of authority for Anglicans.[12] Tradition—as expressed in the councils, creeds, and theologians of the first five centuries of Christianity—and reason are also cited as authoritative: each one necessary and useful for interpreting Scripture. (Scripture, tradition, and reason are authoritative for other Christian traditions as well; although they are not uniquely Anglican, the dynamic interplay among them is often viewed as a distinctive characteristic of Anglican theology.)

The primacy of Scripture is affirmed in historical documents of the Anglican Church. The *Thirty-Nine Articles of Religion*, adopted in 1563 by the Canterbury Convocation, were written to clarify the doctrines of the Church of England as differentiated from Calvinist and Roman Catholic teaching and practices. They assert the primacy of Scripture: "Holy Scripture containeth all things necessary to salvation: so that whatsoever is not read therein, nor may be proved thereby, is not to be required of anyone, that it should be believed as an article of the Faith, or be thought requisite or necessary to salvation."[13]

In 1886, the House of Bishops of the Episcopal Church in the United States issued the *Chicago Lambeth Quadrilateral*, an important document in ongoing ecumenical conversations. It identifies four aspects of Anglican identity shared with Roman Catholic and

Orthodox communions, assigning first place to our common under-standing of the "Holy Scriptures of the Old and New Testaments as the revealed Word of God."[14]

Perhaps nowhere is the primacy of Scripture for Anglicans more clearly seen than in Anglican liturgy. Since Archbishop of Canter-bury Thomas Cranmer introduced the first *Book of Common Prayer* in 1549, every liturgical service in Anglican prayer books includes lectionary readings from the Old Testament, New Testament, and Psalter. Liturgies for the ordination of a priest or bishop require the ordinand or bishop-elect to make a public declaration in the presence of the ordaining bishops and congregation: "I do solemnly declare that I do believe the Holy Scriptures of the Old and New Testament to be the Word of God, and to contain all things neces-sary for salvation." They then sign the declaration in the sight of all present. Immediately following the laying on of hands, a newly ordained deacon, priest, or bishop is given a Bible as a symbol of his or her authority to preach the Word of God and to administer the Holy Sacraments.[15]

The primacy of Scripture has also been reflected in the academic curriculum of Anglican theological schools. While all include course work in the classical theological disciplines of Scripture, church his-tory, liturgics, theology, and ethics, as well as courses in pastoral and practical theology, the balance has often been tipped in favor of a heavier concentration of biblical studies. Emphasis is placed on both the critical study of biblical texts as the revealed Word of God and on the proclamation of the Word and work of God in the world through preaching.

For the 1549 *Book of Common Prayer*, Thomas Cranmer wrote a collect that continues to be read and prayed in Anglican churches throughout the Communion. It speaks of the ways in which the texts of Hebrew and Christian Scriptures both instruct and form us: "Blessed Lord, who caused all holy Scriptures to be written for our learning: Grant us so to hear them, read, mark, learn, and inwardly digest them, that we may embrace and ever hold fast the blessed hope of everlasting life, which you have given us in our Savior Jesus

Christ; who lives and reigns with you and the Holy Spirit, one God, for ever and ever. Amen."[16]

One of my former colleagues at Virginia Theological Seminary (VTS), a gifted church historian and teacher, compares the formation that occurs in the daily reading of Scripture and the recitation of the Psalms to the work of the Colorado River and its tributaries as they slowly but steadily carved out the Grand Canyon over millions of years, transforming the landscape around it. Anglicans are deeply formed and transformed by reading the daily offices of the *Book of Common Prayer*, each with a lectionary that leads us through the full corpus of Scripture in regular, repetitive cycles, with a daily reading of a portion of the Psalter.

While Anglicans, Roman Catholics, and Protestants all claim the centrality of Scripture in their respective traditions, each has different ways of reading and interpreting Scripture. Like our Roman Catholic and Orthodox brothers and sisters, Anglicans acknowledge the importance of understanding Scripture through the lens of the creeds, councils, and writings of the patristic church. Richard Hooker's sixteenth-century appeal to reason as a necessary and authoritative aid to the interpretation of Scripture is consistent with (and perhaps derived from) the earlier Thomistic understanding of natural law. For Hooker, as for Aquinas, Scripture and reason are both gifts from God, working together with no inherent conflict.

Tradition and reason are often cited as two lenses through which Anglicans have sought to read and interpret Scripture. It is important to note, however, that over the centuries, Anglicans have interpreted—and continue to interpret—Scripture in different ways.[17] Difficulties appear as one begins to consider the different ways in which the terms "tradition" and "reason" are understood and applied to the interpretation of Scripture. And yet, one of the distinctive aspects of the ways in which Anglicans read and interpret Scripture can be found in its tolerance of those differences. As Rowan Greer, a professor of Anglican studies, astutely observed, "The paradox that all read Scripture and yet do so in quite different ways is not surprising or necessarily threatening to Christianity in general or of Anglicanism in particular."[18]

Greer's observation leads to a note about the extent to which an understanding of Anglican comprehensiveness contributes to its distinctive nature. Many Anglican scholars have asserted that one of the marks of Anglican theology is its comprehensiveness, retaining doctrines and practices from both Roman Catholic and Protestant traditions. While the generosity of this "big tent" ecclesiology is appealing to many, others find "comprehensiveness" to be an ambiguous term that suggests a lack of theological clarity and rigor or an invitation to moral laxity. The opening sentences from the Lambeth Conference of 1968 address these concerns: "Comprehensiveness demands agreements on fundamentals, while tolerating disagreement on matters in which Christians may differ without feeling the necessity of breaking communion. . . . It is not a sophisticated word for syncretism. Rather, it implies that the apprehension of truth is a growing thing: we only gradually succeed in 'knowing the truth.'"[19]

Despite the ambiguities, many people have been drawn to Anglicanism by its willingness to accept that people of deep faith and good intentions, reflecting theologically and prayerfully on important issues and appealing to the same sources of authority, may disagree with one another and yet remain in conversation and communion.

Another Anglican conviction is the belief that Scripture should be read in community—not just the local community of the reader's congregation, diocese, or country, but within the wider context of a global community of Anglicans, other Christians, and interfaith communities. Reading Scripture together across geographical, denominational, and interfaith divides enables one to understand sacred texts through the eyes and experiences of others.

IV. The Anglican Communion

The Episcopal Church in the United States and the Anglican Church of Canada are two of thirty-eight provinces of the worldwide Anglican Communion. Each has its own autonomous governance structure and primate, and all are members of a global network of local churches in Europe. With this demographic shift, the Anglican Communion has become far more racially, ethnically, and culturally diverse.

Diversity within the Anglican Communion manifests itself in many ways, creating both challenges and opportunities for theological education. One of the primary challenges, as well as opportunities, arises when Anglicans talk with one another about the interpretation and authority of Scripture.

Conflicts have arisen within the Anglican Communion over the past forty years, precipitated by the ordination of women in several provinces and the ordination of gay and lesbian priests and bishops in the United States. Divisions have been sharp enough for some to wonder if the "bonds of affection"[20] that have traditionally connected members of the Communion could be sustained. In 2009, recognizing the questions these issues raised about the authority of Scripture, the Anglican Consultative Council initiated a project titled the Bible in the Life of the Church.[21] Over a period of three years, Anglican scholars from different countries, working closely with the Anglican Communion's Department for Theological Studies, engaged in Bible study with Anglicans in several different provinces. Its purpose was to encourage the practice of reading Scripture in the context of local churches that are part of a larger global community: "The practice of 'reading Scripture together across the Communion' is important because it confronts us with our history and challenges us to work consciously out of our diversity. . . . The primary aim is not agreement, either on the proper interpretation of texts or on how they should figure in the process of moral discernment. . . . Rather, the experience of those who gather around texts over a sustained period is that serious engagement fosters mutual trust and respect, and frequently friendship."[22]

Life in the Anglican Communion requires its members to grapple with the context in which their theology is developed, lived, and taught. In 1972 Desmond Tutu, who would later become Archbishop of Capetown in South Africa, accepted a position in the Theological Education Fund (TEF) of the World Council of Churches, a position he describes as one of the most formative periods of his life. As the associate regional director for Africa, his job was to help fund and improve theological education in training institutions throughout sub-Saharan Africa. Based in London but constantly traveling throughout Africa, Tutu worked with colleagues responsible for work in Latin America, Southeast Asia, Northeast Asia, and the Pacific, each having an associate director from the area to which he was assigned. The staff's diversity was increased by the fact that the director and the four associate directors were all from different Christian denominations.

Over a three-year period, Tutu traveled through twenty-five African countries, often during periods of great political and civic unrest. Many were young nations trying to establish their independence after years of colonial rule, often containing a mixture of people from different cultures or tribes, speaking different languages, and practicing different religions. It was during this time, Tutu has said, that his theological understanding underwent profound changes as he worked within the TEF's framework of contextual theology. It was then that he began to understand how deeply theology is shaped by the different historical, sociological, and cultural contexts in which it is developed.[23] Working in this environment, Tutu began to develop and articulate much of the theology that would inform his future work in South Africa following his return to Johannesburg as the first black dean in 1975. It was there that he first began to speak out against apartheid, work that would consume his time and energy for thirty years and change forever the face of South Africa.

V. Worship: Liturgy as Formation and Transformation

Cranmer's 1549 *Book of Common Prayer* established common patterns and liturgies for daily and weekly worship throughout the Church of

England (and later among provinces throughout the Anglican Communion), making it a sign of unity among its members. Although Cranmer's prayer book has been revised many times and by different geographical provinces throughout the centuries, it retains much of its original structure and content and is a primary text for Anglican theology as well as worship.[24] Liturgy continues to be one of the most distinctive and formative expressions of Anglican identity and mission. As such, worship always occupies a central place in theological education for Anglicans.

Liturgy is the work of the people praising God. It is also the term used for the church's sacramental rites and texts used in public worship. Liturgy plays a significant role in the theological, pedagogical, spiritual, and moral formation of individuals and their faith communities. Wherever Anglicans gather, worship is a central activity in their time together. Samuel Wells has described the many ways that Anglican liturgy contributes to the spiritual and moral formation of worshippers. His essay "How Common Worship Forms Local Character" leads readers through a typical Anglican worship service, noting the ways that each part of the liturgy offers instruction on what it means to be a Christian, shaping not only the theology of worshipers but also their moral formation. A brief excerpt illustrates Wells's reflections on the formative power of the liturgy: "In the simple act of gathering and naming the presence of God, worshippers are not only reminded that they are in the presence of God, but they also develop the faculty of wonder. They have their imaginations stretched to perceive the greatness of God, the mystery of his deciding to make himself known, and the grace of his means of doing so. They are formed in the virtue of humility."[25]

Anglican liturgy is a complex set of activities always greater than the sum of its parts. Sacramental in nature, it is first and foremost the worship of God and a medium for a personal and communal encounter with the divine. It is also a feast for the senses: the place where sights, sounds, smells, touch, and taste all awaken us to the paradoxical mystery of both the transcendence and the nearness of God. Aesthetics are important in Anglican worship, where music, sacred art, architecture, and poetry are incorporated into liturgies that lift the sights of worshippers to "the beauty of holiness." Liturgy enables human beings to transcend the limits of both space and time and see the world not only as it is but as it should be. As Charles Price and Louis Weil described this cosmic dimension, "Liturgy not only implies the transformation of time, but the transformation of worshipers, and finally the transformation of the world."[26]

Perhaps most important for the future, worship is the portal through which most people enter the church and one of the first ways they come to know God. Worship is also a call to service and mission. Worship that is untethered from the church's mission, even when it is aesthetically beautiful, becomes an end unto itself, losing its power to inspire worshippers to work for God's kingdom on earth.

VI. The Mission of the Church

In 1881 Immanuel Chapel was built in the center of the VTS campus. Each weekday the faculty, students, and visitors to the campus gathered for morning worship. A large, beautiful stained-glass window occupied and illuminated the wall behind the altar. It depicted Jesus, just before his Ascension, surrounded by his disciples, giving his final instructions. Around the pointed arch of the window were painted the words "O Ye into All the World and Preach the Gospel." For 129 years, the seminary community was reminded each day that mission stands at the heart of the church, and mission should always be at the center of theological education.

The 1881 chapel was destroyed by fire in 2010. After the fire, planning began for a new chapel. The new Immanuel Chapel was designed and built with a freestanding altar with seating on all four sides, no stained-glass windows, and no ornamentation on the walls. Generations of former students whose ministries had been shaped by this missionary charge insisted that the new chapel should continue to bear witness to the words that were so deeply etched into their minds and hearts. After much discussion (and against the wishes of the architect), the words "GO YE INTO ALL THE WORLD AND PREACH THE GOSPEL" are now painted on the wall behind the baptismal font, an ongoing reminder that theological education must always be in service to the mission of the church.

In the nineteenth century, many graduates of Episcopal seminaries embarked on missionary journeys overseas, preaching the gospel, introducing Anglican liturgies, and establishing schools and congregations in South America, Asia, and Africa. Intentions were honorable, and much good was done, but as TEAC acknowledged, Anglicans have become "keenly aware that our common life and engagement in God's mission are tainted with shortcomings and failures, such as negative aspects of colonial heritage, self-serving abuse of power and privilege, undervaluing of the contributions of laity and women, inequitable distribution of resources, and blindness to the experience of the poor and oppressed."[27]

Painfully aware of these shortcomings and failures, Anglicans no longer view mission as the imposition of a particular way of life on other cultures. Instead, brothers and sisters from other countries, cultures, and religious backgrounds are encouraged to share their stories, traditions, worship, and witness so that all might learn from one another. The presence of students from Africa, Asia, and South America has added an important dimension to theological education for Anglicans in the United States, Canada, and Britain. At the same time, there has been a growing awareness of the mission field that exists just beyond the doors of churches here in America.

VII. The Future of Anglican Theological Education

Previous sections of this essay have described ways in which Scripture, liturgy, and mission have contributed to the development of Anglican theology since the English Reformation. In significant ways, they also set an agenda for the future of Anglican theological education. The "Anglican Way" is defined not only by the presence of these three fundamental commitments but also by the ways in which each supports and reinforces the others within the context of a worldwide Communion that is itself a fourth essential aspect of Anglican identity. For that reason, it will be helpful to note ways in which interplay among these historic commitments can provide a vision for Anglican theological education in rapidly changing times.

The Episcopal Church's Office of Research has created "Transforming Churches," a series of case studies that provides an in-depth analysis of Episcopal congregations in many different geographical locations and cultural contexts that have succeeded in either reversing decline or experiencing substantial growth, finding ways to thrive and carry out their mission in the twenty-first century.[28] Some of these congregations are small; some are large, but each has experienced a renewed sense of identity, mission, and vitality by understanding the social and cultural context in which it is located and paying careful attention to the needs and concerns of their communities. In every instance, having a clear sense of mission and then adapting liturgies and programs to articulate and reinforce the mission have led to congregational renewal, opening church doors to new constituents.

Recent research data confirm the connection between a church's sense of mission and purpose and its potential for growth:

> Important to the growth profile of a congregation are the religious character of the congregation and its sense of mission and purpose. Churches that are clear about why they exist and what they should be doing are most likely to grow. They do not grow because they have been at their location for a century or two or because they have an attractive building where they worship. They grow because they understand their reason for being and make sure they do the things well that are essential to their lives as communities of faith. Without a clear purpose, congregations often resemble inward looking clubs where a fellowship among friends is the primary reason for being. . . . Growth is very unlikely if a church has no definable purpose (other than existing) or if it takes its purpose for granted.[29]

This research has clear implications for Anglican theological schools. Those preparing for congregational leadership, whether lay or ordained, must learn how to "read" and understand the cultural context of their churches in much the same way that Desmond Tutu learned the different cultural contexts of the twenty-five African countries assigned to his oversight in his work at the Theological Education Fund. Not everyone can live or work in such a diverse environment, but theological education within the Anglican Communion must provide opportunities for students to engage in contextual education: learning to read Scripture and do theology in multicultural, global partnerships among seminaries and dioceses throughout the Anglican Communion make it possible for American students to engage in cross-cultural experiences where they may, for the first time in their lives, understand what it is to be the stranger and outsider.

Data from the Episcopal Church's Office of Research also report a strong connection between liturgy and the potential for church growth. Churches that offer more than one Sunday worship service are more likely to grow. Only 15 percent of churches with one Sunday service grew between 2009 and 2013, compared to 38 percent of congregations with four or more services. Since very few churches have four or more services, the key finding is that churches with only one service are not likely to grow, but churches with two or more services are more likely to experience growth. Churches that have more than one "nontypical" service such as Taizé, candlelight services with chant and meditation, or "family-oriented" services followed by a meal are also more likely to grow, as are congregations that hold services in a language other than English—either fully in another language or a bilingual service. Seventy percent of those churches were growing and only 13 percent declining.[30]

Liturgy is always a powerful tool in Anglican churches, but it can no longer be confined to a single expression, especially as local communities become more diverse. It used to be said that an Episcopalian could walk into an Episcopal church anywhere in America and feel at home, hearing the familiar words of the *Book of Common Prayer*. While some are still drawn to the stately cadences of Elizabethan English, others are eager to express their faith in ways that reflect their own cultural heritage and values. Many Episcopal congregations are finding that millennials especially are drawn to liturgies that incorporate a variety of ancient and modern liturgical and musical resources, often coupled with periods of silence and quiet contemplation that provide a welcome respite from a noisy and chaotic world. Anglicans have a rich heritage of such resources from which to draw, not only from its British roots, but also from Africa, New Zealand, and other provinces of the Anglican Communion. Liturgy, when aligned with mission, has much to offer a generation of young adults who have a global perspective, who consider themselves "spiritual, but not religious," who care deeply about environmental issues, and who want to make a difference in the world, all characteristics of millennials.[31]

Continuity amid Change

Demographic data make it clear that the Episcopal Church can no longer support ten residential seminaries, nor can any single model of education and formation suffice for the current and futures needs of the church and its ministries. Given these realities, as new educational models are being developed, it is important to preserve the distinctive aspects of Anglicanism that can respond to the questions, concerns, and spiritual yearnings of our time.

TEAC reminds us that theological education and formation for ministry is the work of the whole church, available to all the faithful, and not just the work of a handful of regional seminaries whose primary focus is on ordained ministry. This is not a new idea but one that needs to be more widely implemented. In 1975 the School of Theology of the University of the South developed a comprehensive four-year curriculum for laity that includes study of Scripture, church history, theology, and ethics. Students meet weekly in small groups with a mentor for worship, discussion of assigned readings, and theological reflection. Education for Ministry (EfM) has enrolled more than eighty thousand participants in the United States and many other countries throughout the world, greatly increasing biblical and theological literacy among participants and preserving an Anglican commitment to the importance of rigorous intellectual inquiry and theological reflection. Its rhythm of study, prayer, worship, and fellowship preserves the traditional components of Anglican formation within a locally based, nonresidential theological education curriculum. In some places, EfM has also become a model for the education and formation of bivocational clergy, deacons whose ministries are primarily in the secular world, and other church professionals.

Other new educational models are being created or strengthened for preparing clergy in nonresidential settings. Low residency programs allow students to take most of their courses online, with two brief periods of residency each year at a theological school, a model that significantly reduces the financial cost to students and the amount of staff and facilities required by schools. Hybrid models combine distance learning with local internships in churches where clergy and lay leaders provide training in the development of liturgical, pastoral, homiletic, and other ministerial skills. These programs are not unlike the model of Anglican formation in colonial America, when candidates for ordination "read divinity" with a local cleric or bishop, then spent two or three years as a curate in a congregation under the supervision of the rector. Regional alternative training programs continue to be developed in various geographical locations in response to local needs.[32] New partnerships are also being developed between Episcopal seminaries no longer able to sustain a full-time residential program and theological schools of other denominations. The creation of Anglican houses of study within these schools makes it possible to retain an Anglican ethos in academic settings that are larger, more diverse, and more ecumenical than most Episcopal seminaries.

Residential seminaries will continue to play a significant role in the life of the Episcopal Church and Anglican Communion. In addition to preserving a traditional model of ministerial formation within a residential community, these schools have an important convening role. They bring people together for lectures, continuing education programs, and meetings of local, diocesan, national, and international working groups. Full-time residential faculty not only teach but also engage in academic research and writing that advances scholarship for the church and its members, encouraging thoughtful and critical reading of the texts and traditions of Christianity and its Anglican expression. Residential space makes it possible to welcome visiting scholars and church leaders from other parts of the Communion or other religious traditions. Hospitality to these visitors facilitates important conversations about the mission of the church, helping resident faculty to understand the challenges facing clergy and congregations and strengthening relationships between theological schools and their denominational structures. The experience of residential students and faculty is greatly enriched by the opportunity to interact with guests who often join the community for daily worship, meals, and informal conversation.

Each of these models creates opportunities for a curriculum that reflects traditional Anglican values and practices. Any new vision for Anglican theological education should reflect the specific connections that TEAC has made between the work of theological education and the Marks of Mission of the Anglican Communion, a statement that expresses the Communion's common commitment to and understanding of God's mission in the world. The five Marks of Mission are

- to proclaim the Good News of the Kingdom;
- to teach, baptize, and nurture new believers;
- to respond to human need by loving service;
- to seek to transform unjust structures of society, to challenge violence of every kind and pursue peace and reconciliation;
- to strive to safeguard the integrity of creation and sustain and renew the life of the earth.[33]

All these Marks of Mission have relevance for an Anglican course of study in which Scripture, theology, ethics, homiletics, liturgics, pastoral theology, and leadership development are integrated into the academic curriculum. Each also suggests a range of pedagogical questions that invite students to "think with the church" to fashion a distinctly Anglican response to the most vexing and complex questions of their time. Theological schools must help students to grapple with these questions as they form leaders who will have the courage and the necessary skills to provide leadership not only in the church but also in civic life and public discourse.

Technology will play a critical role in all-new models of theological education, enabling students to enroll in online distance or distributive educational programs and providing opportunities for Anglicans to interact on a personal level and regular basis with colleagues throughout the Communion. Technology is a tool that can help to bridge cultural gaps among members of the Anglican Communion. Ellen Davis was a member of the Bible in the Life of the Church project and since 2004 has made regular visits to the Diocese of Renk in Southern Sudan, teaching Hebrew Bible and other short courses on theological topics under the auspices of the Episcopal Church of Sudan.[34] She suggests that the most helpful way of building the bonds of affection is to invest in technology so that every Anglican graduate from a theological school can engage in "face time" with Anglicans in other parts of the Communion, noting that such conversations have proven to be highly effective. Establishing personal relationships across geographical and cultural divides creates a context of mutual respect and trust in which participants can share their different perspectives on the interpretation of Scripture and other issues that threaten the unity of the Communion.

Anglican Comprehensiveness

Perhaps the greatest promise for Anglican theological education lies in its long commitment to comprehensiveness. At a time when American society is highly segmented and polarized, with lines of division sharply drawn and fiercely defended, Anglican schools provide places where different perspectives can coexist and be thoughtfully examined. This openness to differences, coupled with Anglicanism's acceptance of ambiguity as an inherent dimension of the human condition and the life of faith, creates a fertile climate for honest theological inquiry and debate.

After a review of the many ways that Anglicans have interpreted Scripture throughout the centuries, Professor Greer concluded that "there is no single approach to Scripture in Anglicanism and no single Anglican theological perspective," nor is there "*the* correct doctrine or *the* correct reading of Scripture." Using the analogy of literary criticism, Greer observed that "we can certainly speak of incorrect interpretations of a poem, but must also recognize a range of valid interpretations which have at least the possibility of being complementary."[35] The willingness of Anglicans to recognize multiple theological perspectives, acknowledging the validity of those that differ from their own, counters the insistence of those who maintain that there is only one way to be a faithful Christian. Anglican comprehensiveness encourages religious freedom and tolerance in a world that too often has witnessed violent atrocities incited by religious extremists seeking to impose their faith on others.

Anglican comprehensiveness is also expressed in the preservation of a religious heritage that encompasses Roman Catholic, Orthodox, and Reformed traditions. It does so not as an act of compromise but as an expression of respect for the unique charisms each has contributed to the greater Christian community. It also creates a via media for those seeking to be part of a Christian faith community but finding themselves unable to embrace some of the doctrines and practices of Roman Catholic, Orthodox, or evangelical Protestant Christianity. Anglicanism is neither a conflation of these different expressions of Christianity nor a patchwork quilt of eclectic practices borrowed from other traditions but rather its own unique expression of the "Anglican Way" of being Christian as articulated in the "Signpost" statement cited and described in this essay. Its vision of a spacious ecclesial tent that invites, welcomes, and accommodates

Christians from different backgrounds and theological perspectives is meant to reflect the vision of the heavenly church described in the book of Revelation, the "great multitude that none can count, from every nation, from all tribes and people and languages, standing before the throne of God" (Rev. 7:9–12).

3

THE ECCLESIAL VISION OF POPE FRANCIS AND THE FUTURE OF CATHOLIC THEOLOGICAL EDUCATION
Donald Senior, CP

Predictably, any reflection on Roman Catholic seminaries or centers of theological education will have to take into account official church guidelines that inform preparation for both ordained ministry and now lay ministry. There are a variety of levels of ministry in Roman Catholicism today and various modes of preparation: deacons typically go through a two- or three-year training program sponsored by a diocese; lay ecclesial ministers (who might serve as pastoral associates or directors of religious education and other professional roles) obtain either a master of divinity or an equivalent degree at a school of theology or university or else participate in nondegree diocesan-sponsored programs; the hosts of lay volunteers in parishes may be trained within the parish or participate in various workshops and courses sponsored by the diocese or provided by nearby seminaries or universities.

However, preparation for ordained priesthood remains the paradigm and dominant reference point in discussions of Catholic theological education and is the focus of most formal Catholic directives. The focus of this chapter is on seminary preparation for ordained ministry, but the values proposed will apply as well to preparation for Catholic ministry at all levels.

I. The Dominant Influence of *Pastores Dabo Vobis*

One of the most influential statements on priestly formation was the 1992 work of Pope John Paul II, titled *Pastores Dabo Vobis* (the Latin title is a quotation from Jeremiah 3:15, "I will give you pastors after my own heart"). The statement was a formal response to a General Synod of Bishops from around the world that had met in Rome in 1990 on the subject of priestly formation and had offered the pope a series of recommendations. The central message of the document was to identify four essential dimensions of priestly formation. These four dimensions or aspects have been cited in virtually every document on Catholic theological education that has appeared in the years since the pope's formulation.[1]

1. The human dimension. The pope explained that a candidate for priesthood should have a mature human capacity for pastoral work:

> Future priests should therefore cultivate a series of human qualities, not only out of proper and due growth and realization of self, but also with a view to the ministry. These qualities are needed for them to be balanced people, strong and free, capable of bearing the weight of pastoral responsibilities. They need to be educated to love the truth, to be loyal, to respect every person, to have a sense of justice, to be true to their word, to be genuinely compassionate, to be men of integrity and, especially, to be balanced in judgment and behavior. . . . Of special importance is the capacity to relate to others. This is truly fundamental for a person who is called to be responsible for a community and to be a "man of communion." This demands that the priest not be arrogant, or quarrelsome, but affable, hospitable, sincere in his words and heart, prudent and discreet, generous and ready to serve, capable of opening himself to clear and brotherly relationships and of encouraging the same in others, and quick to understand, forgive and console (cf. 1 Tm. 3:1–5; Ti. 1:7–9). People today are often trapped in situations of standardization and loneliness, especially in large urban centers, and they become ever more appreciative of the value of communion. Today this is one of the

most eloquent signs and one of the most effective ways of transmitting the Gospel message. In this context affective maturity, which is the result of an education in true and responsible love, is a significant and decisive factor in the formation of candidates for the priesthood.[2]

Significantly, the pope emphasized that this human dimension was foundational for everything else. Neither spirituality, intellectual brilliance, nor pastoral training could substitute for it.

2. The spiritual dimension. Human formation, the pope noted, leads to a proper spiritual formation: "In this bond between the Lord Jesus Christ and the priest, an ontological and psychological bond, a sacramental and moral bond, is the foundation and likewise the power for that 'life according to the Spirit' and 'radicalism of the Gospel' to which every priest is called today and which is fostered by ongoing formation in its spiritual aspect."[3] Here the document stresses the need for a life of prayer, of immersion in the Scriptures, and of cultivating the spiritual disciplines that lead to a life of holiness. "And just as for all the faithful spiritual formation is central and unifies their being and living as Christians, that is, as new creatures in Christ who walk in the Spirit, so too for every priest his spiritual formation is the core which unifies and gives life to his being a priest and his acting as a priest."[4]

3. The intellectual dimension. Here the pope stressed the importance of appropriating knowledge of Scripture and the church's authentic theological tradition. "As one who shares in the prophetic mission of Jesus and is part of the mystery of the church, the teacher of truth, the priest is called to reveal to others, in Jesus Christ, the true face of God, and as a result the true face of humanity."[5] This intellectual grounding, the pope noted, was especially important for the priest's ministry of the word: "The commitment to study, which takes up no small part of the time of those preparing for the priesthood, is not in fact an external and secondary dimension of their human, Christian, spiritual and vocational growth. In reality, through study, especially the study of theology, the future priest assents to the word of God, grows in his spiritual life and prepares himself to fulfill his pastoral ministry. . . . To be pastorally effective, intellectual formation is to be integrated with a spirituality marked by a personal experience of God. In this way a purely abstract approach to knowledge is overcome in favor of that intelligence of heart which knows how 'to look beyond,' and then is in a position to communicate the mystery of God to the people."[6]

4. The pastoral dimension. The entire purpose of theological education for priesthood is pastoral: "The whole formation imparted to candidates for the priesthood aims at preparing them to enter into communion with the charity of Christ the good shepherd. Hence their formation in its different aspects must have a fundamentally pastoral character. . . . Just as all the Lord's activity was the fruit and sign of pastoral charity, so should the priest's ministerial activity be. Pastoral charity is a gift, but it is likewise a task, a grace and a responsibility to which we must be faithful."[7] To achieve this, the candidate needs to develop the skill to discern the real situations of the men and women to whom he is sent and to be schooled in the pastoral skills and methods required to meet the spiritual needs of the people.

The key, of course, for effective priestly training is the integration of all four of these dimensions within the academic curriculum and formation program of the seminary or school of theology. This framework, by the way, had a decisive influence on the guidelines for seminary training produced by the United States Conference of Catholic Bishops. The *Program for Priestly Formation*, now in its fifth (2005) edition, was compiled in consultation with the US bishops, major superiors of religious orders, and the leadership of the US seminary community. In addition to endorsing the fourfold framework for formation enunciated by Pope John Paul II cited earlier, it also outlines the fundamental curricular content required for priestly ordination. A subsequent United States Conference of Catholic Bishops document, titled *Co-workers in the Vineyard of the Lord* (1995), also provided direction for the formation of lay ecclesial ministers and drew on the general tenor of these guidelines for priestly formation.[8]

To a certain extent, the fourfold dimensions presented in *Pastores Dabo Vobis* are perennial and inevitable categories. It is hard to imagine any program of theological education, present or future, that would not in some fashion include these dimensions. Yet they are also very generic and need further definition. They also have to be adapted to a variety of educational formats and structures now beginning to emerge in theological education. While Roman Catholicism still holds tightly to the classic form of preparation for ordained ministry (i.e., graduate education that is the equivalent of the master of divinity degree, in a residential program, and with intense spiritual formation), there are some adaptations taking place, particularly in the formal preparation of Catholic lay ecclesial ministers such as online courses and online formation programs, particularly for the many dioceses in the United States that do not have access to seminary or university programs.

Even more important—and challenging—is to consider the particular values and accents that are included under each of these four dimensions. Human formation, yes, but what are the specific human qualities and skills most urgently needed for the church and its future? Spiritual and pastoral formation, yes, but what is the ecclesial vision that guides the tone and content of such formation? Intellectual formation, yes, but what are some of the moral and scientific issues that will face the church of the future and require the adaptation or reinterpretation of its theological language and categories?

II. THE ECCLESIAL VISION OF POPE FRANCIS

It is at this point that I would like turn to the current pope, Pope Francis, to attempt to gaze into the future of Catholic theological education through the lens of his compelling vision of the church. In my view, Pope Francis has captured, both in his symbolic actions and his major writings, the enduring biblical and Christian values that must inform theological education for the future. In Pope Francis, we have a pope who has thoroughly absorbed the pastoral spirit of Vatican II, the missionary experience of Latin America and its accent on a theology of liberation, and a profoundly human and compassionate way of relating to others. I believe that in drawing on his vision of the church, a vision grounded in Scripture and Catholic tradition as well as in contemporary experience, the enduring values that must inform theological education of the future can be found.

Pope Francis's vision of the church and its emerging needs are spelled out in three major documents that have marked his relatively short papacy and reflect his unique pastoral style: (1) *Evangelii Gaudium* (*The Joy of the Gospel*), his 2013 document on evangelization; (2) *Laudato Si'* (*On Care for Our Common Home*), his 2015 innovative statement on ecology; and (3) *Amoris Laetitia* (*The Joy of Love*), his 2016 statement on marriage and family. Cumulatively, these statements offer a compelling portrayal of the church and its mission that I believe offers a path for the future of Catholic theological education.

Evangelii Gaudium (The Joy of the Gospel)

The pope's statement on evangelization, while formally a response to the recommendations of the bishops' general synod of 2012 on this topic, turned out to be a manifesto or overall blueprint for his own papal ministry.[9] Written in his typical passionate, direct, and sometimes poetic style, the statement begins at the heart of the matter. Evangelization, the pope insists, is rooted in a personal encounter with Jesus Christ, for which there is no substitute for anyone who aspires to proclaim the gospel. The pope also notes that the encounter with Jesus, who embodies God's own unconditional love for the world and whose mission of teaching and healing were animated by self-transcending love culminating in the giving of his own life for others, coincides with the deepest instinct and expression of mature human life—namely, the capacity to move beyond oneself and relate with generosity and love with the other. As Pope Francis puts it, "Life grows by being given away, and it weakens in isolation and comfort. Indeed, those who enjoy life most are those who leave security on the shore and become excited by the mission of communicating life to others."[10]

This leads, in turn, to the pope's question: What would a community made up of those rooted in the love of Christ look like? His answer—one that has characterized virtually every statement he has made subsequently about the church—is that it is to be a community of "missionary disciples," a "communion" of those who are called to follow Christ and to take up his mission to the world—that is, not a church turned in on itself but one turned outward to the world in love and mercy and service. Right from the beginning of his Petrine ministry, Pope Francis in both word and symbolic gesture has pointed to this essential missional and outward-directed nature of the church. Before the election of the pope, the college of cardinals had gathered in Rome for a few days to reflect together on the challenges facing the church and the new pope. When Cardinal Bergolio's turn to speak came, he told the popular story of Jesus knocking on the door of the church. In most versions of this story, the idea is that Jesus is knocking on the door, trying to enter into a church that lacks his presence. In Bergolio's version, he said perhaps Jesus was knocking on the door of the church in order *to get out*, out into the world to love it and serve it![11]

His own pastoral outreach since he became pope has driven home this perspective. The church, he believes, had become too turned in on itself, too clerical, too absorbed with domestic issues. Thus as pope, he has consistently reached out to the poor; to the immigrants and refugees; to people of other religious traditions; to scientists, humanists, and nonbelievers. He, in turn, has challenged his fellow bishops and priests to be close to their people, as he vividly notes, "to smell like the sheep" and not to be aloof or to project a sour disposition, as he memorably notes, "looking like someone who just came back from a funeral."

The remaining sections of the *Joy of the Gospel* elaborate on this fundamental intuition about the church. The "language" of the church and its ministers is to be "dialogical" and respectful, not imperial or arrogant. The church should foster a "culture of encounter," moving away from dogmatism and abstract moral condemnations. Proclamation of the gospel, the pope insists, is the responsibility of the whole church, not just clergy: "All the baptized, whatever their position in the church or their level of instruction in the faith, are agents of evangelization, and it would be insufficient to envisage a plan of evangelization to be carried out by professionals while the rest of the faithful would simply be passive recipients."[12] At the same time, the pope urged ordained priests and deacons to invest more effort in effective preaching as a prime mode of evangelization. One of the unusual features of the pope's statement is the detailed attention he gives to the ministry of preaching.[13] His comments even include specific instructions on how to prepare a homily and how to structure it. (It should be noted that, in fact, Pope Francis himself is recognized as a very effective preacher, offering a biblically based homily each morning before a congregation of ordinary people, drawn from the families of Vatican workers and random visitors.[14])

From a reflection on the universal call to proclaim the gospel that is the responsibility of all the baptized, the pope turns to the social dimensions of the church's evangelization. The pope cites particular areas of the church's outward mission that he believes are most urgent. First of all is the church's need to pursue justice, particularly on behalf of the poor and vulnerable. For the pope, solidarity with the poor and suffering is the touchstone of authentic Christianity. As he observes, "For the Church, the option for the poor is primarily a theological category rather than a cultural, sociological, political or philosophical one." God shows the poor "his first mercy" (a quote from his predecessor John Paul II). The church's commitment to the poor is a two-way street:

> That is why I want a Church which is poor and for the poor. They have much to teach us. Not only do they share in the *sensus fidei*, but in their difficulties they know the suffering Christ. We need to let ourselves be evangelized by them. The new evangelization is an invitation to acknowledge the saving power at work in their lives and to put them at the center of the Church's pilgrim way.

We are called to find Christ in them, to lend our voice to their causes, but also to be their friends, to listen to them, to speak for them and to embrace the mysterious wisdom which God wishes to share with us through them.[15]

The challenge to the developed nations of the world regarding economic inequity has become a hallmark of Pope Francis's preaching and teaching, fortified with his own actions—for example, early on, visiting the site where so many refugees lost their lives at the Italian port of Lesbos, welcoming the poor and homeless of Rome into his own residence and sharing a meal with them, offering sanctuary for several refugee families within the Vatican itself, setting up showers for the homeless next to St. Peter's, visiting Muslim prisoners in Rome and washing their feet during the Holy Thursday liturgy, hosting a prayer of reconciliation with the leaders of Israel and Palestine, and so on.

In pointing to the social dimension of evangelization, Pope Francis also singles out the church's mission of "reconciliation" and peacemaking as a prime expression of its missionary nature but includes under that a variety of dimensions. Where appropriate, he notes, the church and its leaders should be available to help facilitate conflicts between nations and groups, despite the risks of being involved politically. A spirit of peacemaking and reconciliation should also prompt the church to reach across boundaries to engage in dialogue with the scientific community and people who represent a secular and humanist perspective in seeking to build up the common good. Likewise, the church's mission of peace and reconciliation should drive its unyielding commitment to ecumenism and interfaith relations.

In all this, the stance of the church is to be humble, respectful, and dialogical.

Laudato Si' (On Care for Our Common Home)

Other aspects of Pope Francis's ecclesial vision emerge in his encyclical letter on ecology. The title *Laudato Si'*, old Italian for "praise you," is taken from St. Francis of Assisi (whose name the pope deliberately chose) and his striking "Canticle of Creation."[16] Built on extensive consultation with the scientific community (exemplifying his call for dialogue with science in *The Joy of the Gospel*), the pope expands the moral horizon of the church to include respect for the earth and the universe itself. The shocking level of pollution and other damage to the environment now observable, plus the fact that the most dire consequences of the ecological crisis fall on the poor, must be a warning sign to Christians and to the leadership of the church.

The pope's statements here and in his other declarations are strikingly biblical in tone and substance. *Laudato Si'*, for example, spends considerable time reviewing the biblical theology of creation. Creation is a gift of God's outward flowing love and, as affirmed in Genesis 1, is intrinsically good. The human is responsible to care for the earth, to "till it" and develop it, not exploit it (Gen. 2:15). Harm to the earth and to the human community is a consequence of sin that spills over into arrogance, jealousy, and violence. The fundamental conviction of the Scriptures and of Christian tradition is that humans are essentially interdependent—having foundational and defining relationships with each other, with the earth and the universe, and with God. "Everything is related," the pope notes, "and we human beings are united as brothers and sisters on a wonderful pilgrimage, woven together by the love God has for each of his creatures and which also unites us in fond affection with brother sun, sister moon, brother river and mother earth."[17]

Awareness of this essential interrelated nature of the human being calls for a new level of conversion, one that leads us to consider changes in our very style of life, one that moves away from an obsessive consumerism and develops a sensitivity as to how our values and our way of life affect other human beings and the earth itself. What is needed, the pope states, is "an 'ecological conversion,' whereby the effects of [Christians'] encounter with Jesus Christ become evident in their relationship with the world around them. Living our vocation to be protectors of God's handiwork is essential to a life of virtue; it is not an optional or a secondary aspect of our Christian experience."[18] Allied to this is Pope Francis's encouragement on a number of occasions for those involved in the church's mission to contemplate beauty: "The relationship between a good aesthetic education and the maintenance of a healthy environment cannot be overlooked. By learning to see and appreciate beauty, we learn to reject self-interested pragmatism. If someone has not learned to stop and admire something beautiful, we should not be surprised if he or she treats everything as an object to be used and abused without scruple."[19]

The church's mission is ultimately to "set before the world the ideal of 'a civilization of love.'"[20] "In order to make society more human, more worthy of the human person, love in social life—political, economic and cultural—must be given renewed value, becoming the constant and highest norm for all activity. In this framework, along with the importance of little everyday gestures, social love moves us to devise larger strategies to halt environmental degradation and to encourage a 'culture of care' which permeates all of society."[21] The pope's reference to "little gestures" is explained earlier in his statement. The enormity of the challenges posed by the ecological crisis can lead us to despair or indifference. Such moral numbness can be overcome by a spirit of faith that views the world as intrinsically good and beautiful as a gift of God and by dialogue that enables us to work together with other people of goodwill to find ways to address the ecological crisis. At the same time, each of us is able on a daily basis to do "little" but genuine and effective gestures that express our moral response. Here he cites the spirituality of a famous nineteenth-century Catholic saint, Therese of Lisieux, who spoke of the "little way of love" as a form of authentic Christian spirituality—that is, "not to miss out on a kind word, a smile or any small gesture which sows peace and friendship." The pope goes on to note, "An integral ecology is also made up of simple daily gestures which break with the logic of violence, exploitation and selfishness. . . . Love, overflowing with small gestures of mutual care, is also civic and political, and it makes itself felt in every action that seeks to build a better world."[22]

Amoris Laetitia (The Joy of Love)

The most recent of Pope Francis's statements is titled *Amoris Laetitia*, Latin for *The Joy of Love*, and is subtitled *On Love in the Family*. As was the case for *The Joy of the Gospel*, this was his formal response to the recommendations of the world's bishops' general synod on the family, one that had taken place over two sessions during the course of 2015. This particular synod was in the news because of the public debate within the Catholic community over the controversial issue of the church's pastoral response to divorced and remarried couples. Could such couples return to full communion with the church, including reception of the Eucharist—a long-standing prohibition in Catholic tradition? Pope Francis, to the consternation of some church leaders, welcomed and encouraged such debate. While his formal response is focused on the importance of a healthy family life for both human society and the life of the church, his reflections also had significant implications for the church's approach to a host of contemporary moral issues.

As in his other statements, the pope built his recommendations on a solid biblical foundation. A remarkable part of *Amoris Laetitia* is a chapter titled "Love in Marriage," based on a close word-by-word analysis of Paul's reflection on charity in 1 Corinthians 13:4–7. While noting that Paul speaks here of the bond of love among Christians within the community, the pope adapts the experiential and nonsentimental nature of Paul's reflections to describe the kind of seasoned and enduring love that should characterize the relationship between spouses.

But the most widely discussed section of the pope's statement is found in chapter 8, titled "Accompanying, Discerning and Integrating Weakness." The specific "weakness" pointed to in the context of this document on marriage is the experience of couples who are living together outside of matrimony, or couples whose marriage has failed, or couples who after divorce have remarried and are seeking their way to a full life within the church. In response, the pope reaffirms traditional Catholic teaching on the value and permanence of marriage and the serious consequences of divorce. But he is not content to leave it at that. He urges that couples and their pastoral leaders need to employ serious discernment in determining the prudent and authentically Christian way to respond to particular ambiguous and complex situations.

The most important moral and pastoral principle to keep in mind, he notes, is that of mercy. He observes, "There are two ways of thinking which recur throughout the Church's history: casting off and reinstating. The Church's way, from the time of the Council of Jerusalem, has always been the way of Jesus, the way of mercy and reinstatement. . . . The way of the Church is not to condemn anyone forever; it is to pour out the balm of God's mercy on all those who ask for it with a sincere heart."[23] He concludes, "Consequently, there is a need 'to avoid judgments which do not take into account the complexity of various situations" and "to be attentive, by necessity, to how people experience distress because of their condition."[24] Or again, citing the principle of mercy, "It is a matter of reaching out to everyone, of needing to help each person find his or her proper way of participating in the ecclesial community and thus to experience being touched by 'unmerited, unconditional and gratuitous' mercy."[25]

The role of the priest in response to the pastoral needs of Christians in difficult moral circumstances is "to accompany with mercy and patience the eventual stages of personal growth as these progressively appear. . . . The Church's pastors, in proposing to the faithful the full ideal of the gospel and the Church's teaching, must also help them to treat the weak with compassion, avoiding aggravation or unduly harsh or hasty judgements."[26]

It is clear that in reflecting on the complex situations that face married and remarried couples in today's world, the pope is also expressing a pastoral stance that should characterize the church's approach to all circumstances. In all instances, the instinct of the church of Jesus Christ is to respond with mercy. "Mercy," he notes, "is the beating heart of the Gospel, which in its own way must penetrate the mind and heart of every person."[27] An emphasis on mercy as the defining principle of the church's pastoral response is, he notes, "not sheer romanticism or a lukewarm response to God's love, which always seeks what is best for us, for 'mercy is the very foundation of the Church's life. All of her pastoral activity should be caught up in the tenderness which she shows to believers; nothing in her preaching and her witness to the world can be lacking in mercy.'"[28] This emphasis on mercy and discernment, he concludes, "offers us a framework and a setting which help us avoid a cold bureaucratic morality in dealing with more sensitive issues. Instead, it sets us in the context of a pastoral discernment filled with merciful love, which is ever ready to understand, forgive, accompany, hope, and above all integrate. That is the mindset which should prevail in the church and lead us to open our hearts to those living on the outermost fringes of society."[29]

One of the most famous metaphors Pope Francis has used for the church as a proclaimer of mercy was first expressed in an interview he had in 2013 at the very beginning of his tenure as pope with an Italian journalist, Fr. Anthony Spandaro, editor of the journal *Civiltà Cattolica*: "I can clearly see that what the Church needs today is the ability to heal wounds and warm the hearts of the faithful, it needs to be by their side. I see the Church as a field hospital after a battle. It's pointless to ask a seriously injured patient whether his cholesterol or blood sugar levels are high! It's his wounds that need to be healed. The rest we can talk about later. Now we must think about treating those wounds. And we need to start from the bottom."

III. ECCLESIAL VISION AND THEOLOGICAL EDUCATION

There are any number of challenges facing preparation for ordained and lay ecclesial ministry within the Roman Catholic Church of the future. The number of ordained priests continues to decline, or at best, to remain static, especially in the face of fewer candidates and more retirements. The levels of practice among US Catholics are steadily eroding, especially among younger generations. In a number of major urban dioceses, there is a need for consolidation of parishes because of both declining numbers and demographic shifts that leave many older, center-city parishes underused and contributing to mounting maintenance costs. While many dioceses still cling to their own existing seminary facilities, this has led, in some instances, to student bodies too few in numbers for effective graduate seminary education. These problems are well known by every Catholic Church leader.

The need for radical change in the manner of seminary preparation for ordained ministry has not yet been felt. The vast majority of diocesan seminarians are prepared in traditional residential seminaries. In the case of religious order seminarians, most reside in "formation houses" sponsored by their own communities while attending theologates—either diocesan seminaries or religious-order-sponsored theology schools—for their academic and pastoral training. More innovation has taken place in the preparation of lay ecclesial ministers. Many smaller dioceses have forged relationships with seminaries and religious-order theologates or Catholic universities to provide online theological education while the diocese itself sees to the recruitment and formation of the lay ministers themselves. Consolidation of parishes into "megaparishes" in such places as Florida and elsewhere has prompted some pastors to run their own training programs for the hosts of lay volunteers often involved in the administration and ministerial life of such parishes.

One senses that on a structural and pedagogical level, the Catholic Church in the United States will muddle through for the time being, introducing adaptations when circumstances eventually demand it. But the question remains, What will be the tenor of the preparation for those who will serve the church's mission in a formal way? What values and perspectives will be most life giving for the service of God's people as the future unfolds? What type of candidates will be most suitable for the kind of evangelization that the emerging needs of our world demands? In concluding her recent study of Catholic seminaries, Katarina Schuth summarized her own hope: "My hope for the future rests on theologates making improvements in directions that respond more fully to the spiritual needs in people's lives and the requirements of the new evangelization."[30]

What might those needs and requirements be? Here is where I think the ecclesial vision of Pope Francis can help. His reflections on the church and its mission are not idiosyncratic nor without precedent. Much of what he teaches about the church was affirmed by his predecessors and resonates with the experience of the church throughout the world. His view of the church has deep biblical roots and strong affinity with Catholic tradition. But the current pope has also articulated in a consistent, cogent, and vivid way some of the most urgent emerging needs of our contemporary world and their interface with the deep instincts of the gospel. The elements of his ecclesial vision give new life to the classic fourfold categories of priestly formation.

What does the content of his ecclesial vision suggest for the future of theological education in the Roman Catholic community? What should be the attitudes and pastoral priorities of those who will serve as priests, deacons, or lay ecclesial ministers? How, in other words, would the ecclesial vision enunciated by the pope be translated into the human, spiritual, intellectual, and pastoral formation of future ministers? Allow me to make some suggestions, even if in a rather generic way:

1. On a human level, candidates for the church's ministry will need to have a capacity for relating to others in a deeply empathetic way. This has already been an emphasis of the church's policy, but it needs to be reinforced. A person who demonstrates authoritarian tendencies, whose desire to serve the church is tinged with clerical ambition, who seeks a career in the church, or who is drawn mainly by the opportunity to lead the church's liturgy or to exercise authority in a parish will not be able to carry out the church's evangelization in the spirit of the gospel. This is not to say that candidates have to be strong extroverts; there always has been and ever will be room for a wide variety of personalities and personal styles among the ministers of the gospel. But a love for people and the innate capacity to relate to others in a healthy and sympathetic

way are essential qualities more than ever. A number of candidates for ministry are being drawn from college graduates who during or immediately after their college days have spent significant time in volunteer programs, working with the poor in Latin America, teaching in inner-city schools, and so on. They already demonstrate the respect for others and the inclination to service required for the church's mission. The church described by the pope is itself an outward-directed community, not one absorbed by its own concerns or with domestic ecclesial politics. The pope frequently refers to the church as fostering and expressing a "culture of encounter," which implies that its representatives are willing to engage with respect and care others who may have very different perspectives about life and religion.[31] While some doctrinally rigid church ministers view dialogue as some form of "compromise" to be avoided, the pope insists that an aptitude for dialogue is an essential ecclesial virtue.

2. The candidate for serving in the church's future mission must also exemplify and foster a deep personal relationship with Jesus Christ. This may be self-evident, but it cannot be taken for granted. It is, in fact, a first principle before everything else. At every turn, the pope has emphasized the importance of this faith relationship with Christ as the essential starting point for every aspect of the church's life. There is a strong contemplative bent to the pope's teaching about ministry. In *The Joy of the Gospel*, he urges those involved in the work of evangelization to be rooted in a life of prayer and contemplation: "What is needed is the ability to cultivate an interior space which can give a Christian meaning to commitment and activity. . . . Without prolonged moments of adoration, of prayerful encounter with the word, of sincere conversation with the Lord, our work easily becomes meaningless; we lose energy as a result of weariness and difficulties, and our fervor dies out."[32]

3. The candidate for ministry should also develop an eye for beauty—in nature, in great literature, in poetry and drama. The pope has reflected on this in speaking of the responsibility of the Christian to care for nature. But an eye for beauty also helps create a spirit of sensitivity in any human being. Many observers

today decry the coarseness and insensitivity that is a by-product of the fascination with pornography that is readily available on the internet or the violence that fills so many video games. Time and again we hear of persons who have fed on images of sexual exploitation and violence, treating women and children with contempt and sometimes with destructive violence. Long ago, a novice master I was fortunate to have counseled us to fill our minds and imaginations with images of beauty in all its forms; too soon, he warned, a flood of crude and ugly imagery will attempt to take over our minds and spirits.[33] This is a dimension of formation often overlooked or perhaps even considered superfluous or frivolous but one that may be even more urgent for the future.

I would be very remiss, as one who has taught the New Testament for more than forty years, if I did not mention that immersion in the biblical text is also an experience of beauty. The Scriptures are loaded with vivid metaphors and symbols, filled with paradigmatic stories that capture the heart of our faith. Familiarity with the biblical text not only nourishes our faith and theology but likewise gives our imaginations and our language a wash of pure beauty and rhetorical power. It is hard to imagine a Christian theological curriculum of any age that does not make space for broad and deep exposure to the study of Scripture.

4. Pope Francis has repeatedly warned the leadership of the church at every level, including the College of Cardinals, about the danger of "clericalism," of creating a closed ecclesiastical culture that leads the church to use its energy on petty, domestic concerns at the expense of the urgent worldwide mission of the church. Here is a great challenge to theological education. A valid emphasis on fostering priestly identity that has been a focus of Catholic seminary education has to be balanced with mutual respect for lay ministers as coworkers and with respect and care for the laypeople of the parish and institutions the priest will serve. This also means tempering an overemphasis in some theological literature on the unique role of the priest in the church's mission and the essential difference between the identity and ministry of the priest from all other forms

of ministry within the church. The role of the priest within the life of the Catholic Church is, in fact, singular and vital, but it is not so in isolation from other forms of ministry, nor does it give the priest some kind of exalted spiritual status. In a church that is increasingly dependent on lay ministry at all levels in the administration and direct mission of the church, the overemphasis on the role of the clergy becomes even more untenable.[34]

5. As we noted earlier, a hallmark of Pope Francis's teaching and example has been to urge the church to be a church "of the poor and for the poor." Here too is a touchstone for evaluating a candidate's capacity for future ministry within the church. Does a person have an instinctive sense of empathy, respect, and kindness toward those who are poor and suffering? Does the candidate grasp the meaning of a simple lifestyle, one free from obsession with goods and gadgets? Is there an openness to learn from those that others may judge as useless or failed human beings? This important criterion should have an impact as well on the kind of pastoral placements and practicums that are part of the seminary curriculum. A candidate who is only at home in a middle- or upper-class setting and concentrates his ministerial ambition and experience accordingly will have a difficult time in a church "of and for the poor." Likewise, appropriation of the church's strong social doctrine will need to be a hallmark of the seminary curriculum of the future if the church and its leaders are to address with intelligence and subtlety the vast challenges of economic justice facing the world today and to participate with respect and competence in dialogue with other people of goodwill about possible solutions.

6. Pope Francis's view of the church has also extended the horizon of its mission, emphasizing issues of ecology, issues of dialogue with science concerning the environment, and other issues. Missing from the three papal documents we have reviewed is an explicit treatment of the intellectual dimension of priestly formation. Yet his emphasis on cogent and effective preaching, engagement with complex social issues such as the environment, the challenges posed by the changing nature of the family, the importance of formation

of conscience and discernment—all of these presume a thoughtful appropriation and renewed interpretation of the church's theological and ethical traditions. Similarly, his insistence on the importance of ecumenism and interfaith dialogue (especially with Islam) also calls for the Catholic priest or professional minister to be knowledgeable about their own Catholic tradition in order to play a meaningful role in such dialogue: "True openness involves remaining steadfast in one's deepest convictions, clear and joyful in one's own identity, while at the same time being 'open to understanding those of the other party' and 'knowing that dialogue can enrich each side . . .' Evangelization and interreligious dialogue, far from being opposed, mutually support and nourish one another."[35]

7. As we saw in his exhortation on family and marriage, *Amoris Laetitia*, the pope gives great importance to the pastoral role of helping people form their conscience and accompanying them as they discern their path to a deeper Christian life within the church. The practice of "accompaniment" (which is a special emphasis of Latin American pastoral theology) requires both a spirit of kindness and patience on the part of the priest and a solid knowledge of what is at stake in various pastoral decisions. Here too, given the increasing complexity of family structures and the demands of a technological world, preparation for this aspect of ministry and even practice in the exercise of it should be a component of the intellectual and pastoral training of the priest and other ministers of church.

8. A final and foundational emphasis found throughout the teaching and personal example of Pope Francis is his emphasis on mercy. The face of the church is to be a face of mercy rather than that of a distant moral judge who corrects and condemns human wrongdoing. There is, of course, a prophetic responsibility of the church to confront the toxic evils that wound humanity and to speak out on behalf of the poor and vulnerable. Anyone who follows the speeches of the pope knows he does not hesitate to speak forcefully on such issues. Yet the ultimate and guiding stance of the church, as the pope emphasized in *Amoris Laetitia* and his other statements, is mercy. This emphasis finds its root in what the pope described in *The Joy of the*

Gospel as the foundation of Christian life—namely, a personal relationship with Jesus Christ. Jesus, as the pope eloquently proclaimed in inaugurating the recent "Year of Mercy," is "the human face of the Father's mercy."[36] This fundamental emphasis too should have an impact on the theological curriculum of any Catholic seminary or school of theology: "The teaching of moral theology should not fail to incorporate these considerations [about mercy], for although it is quite true that concern must be shown for the integrity of the church's moral teaching, special care should always be shown to emphasize and encourage the highest and most central values of the Gospel, particularly the primacy of charity as a response to the completely gratuitous offer of God's love."[37]

A specific pastoral practice of the Catholic Church that Pope Francis constantly emphasizes in this regard is the Sacrament of Reconciliation or Penance. He urges priests to expand the opportunities for this sacrament in their parishes and, above all, urges them to make it a place where Christians can experience the full force of God's gracious mercy.

The call for the church to embody God's mercy leads to the final and full vision of the church's mission expressed by Pope Francis. The church, he pleads, should work together with all people of goodwill to sustain the ideal of a "civilization of love." That lofty ideal, to which the human heart aspires, is the polar opposite of the civilization of violence and oppression and exploitation that confronts the human family at every turn. Working toward a civilization of love—a civilization that reflects God's mercy—should be the abiding commitment of the church through gestures large and small, through alliances with other Christians and religious traditions, and in alliance with all people of goodwill.

CONCLUSION

In reflecting on Pope Francis's vision of the church and its mission and in considering some of the possible impact of such a vision on the tenor of theological education, I came to realize that this portrayal of humanity and society runs contrary to the implied portrayal of humanity seeming to prevail in so many political and social circles today: a society in which the poor and vulnerable are respected and served rather than ignored or exploited, a society that realizes its interdependence with all life and therefore takes responsibility for the environment rather than one that denies human responsibility and continues to exploit and pollute the earth for economic gain, a society that builds bridges of understanding and love across barriers of religion and culture and economic status instead of a society that builds walls to separate peoples, a society that welcomes the refugee and the stranger as fellow human beings instead of creating bans to prevent people from finding shelter and the possibility of a new life, a society that cherishes traditions of authentic patriotism and appreciates the bounty and culture of its birthplace as a gift rather than a society that appeals to exaggerated and self-serving nationalism, a society that works for economic equity rather than wasting resources on excessive consumerism and military gain, a society that respects women and men and life in all its forms rather than one that indulges in crude sexual exploitation and disrespect.

To promote such a "civilization of love" in our evolving culture will call for ministers of the gospel who are prepared, courageous, compassionate, imaginative, respectful of differences, willing to dialogue, and patient in building up the Kingdom of God. It will be a particular challenge to proclaim this understanding of the gospel in the context of the Catholic Church in North America. Understandably, the attitudes of many Catholics coincide with the values and perspectives of Americans at large. Some will consider the portrayal of the church reflected in the teaching of Pope Francis to be jarring and even threatening to their way of life. The priests, deacons, and lay ministers who are called to evangelize now and in the future will have to exhibit great respect and love for their people while not losing a commitment to the countercultural dimensions of the gospel of Jesus Christ. How to proclaim the gospel in a way that does not alienate but allures Christians to the fullest expression of their faith life—that will be the challenge for the future, as it has been for the past.

4

BROADENING THE
EVANGELICAL VISION
"Needs" and "Wants" in Theological Education
Richard J. Mouw

Someone once told me a poignant story about what it was like growing up in a rural Mennonite community in Pennsylvania. There were no formal requirements in that community in those days for preparation for pastoral ministry, and the pastors were chosen by the casting of lots. When an older pastor died or was otherwise made incapable of performing his duties, the community would gather to choose his successor. This was always a very tense affair, the person reported. All the men in the community were farmers, and typically none of them really wanted to give up their full-time farming activities in order to take on pastoral responsibilities. The men were clearly nervous when the lots were cast, and the announcing of the person who had been chosen to become the pastor was a dramatic moment. These men were not the types to show strong emotions, but the choosing of a new pastor was the one time that the person could remember seeing a Mennonite farmer shed tears in public. And, the person quickly added, they were not tears of joy!

I know many pastors today who shed tears—in private, at least—about the burdens of ministry. And these are men and women who were not chosen by the casting of lots. They had experienced what they took to be a clear divine call to church ministry, and they willingly engaged in an extensive and costly educational program to prepare themselves for their duties. But over and over again, they complain that their courses of study in theological schools did not prepare them adequately for what they actually face today in ministry.

Of course, those kinds of laments have always been expressed. Often in the past, they took the form of complaints about the specific contents of a seminary education. Some courses were seen as a waste of time, and there were other courses that pastors wished their seminaries had included in the curriculum. And those criticisms always had at least some element of legitimacy. There has been a constant temptation in theological education for scholars to pursue interests that are not very helpful to those who face the very real challenges that must be wrestled with on the front lines of ministry.

But these days, the complaints are not simply about how folks wish they could revise the typical seminary curriculum. They often focus, as they have in some times past, on the need for seminary education as such. This is certainly true in the evangelical movement. The antiseminary sentiment was driven home to me in a blunt manner when I was invited during the 1990s to meet with a small group of pastors of large (two-thousand-plus members) congregations. None of these pastors had graduated from a seminary, but a Fuller colleague who had consulted with several of them on "church growth" topics arranged for me to meet with them to talk about possible ties between their ministries and our seminary's programs.

The conversation was not a positive one. Most of it consisted of complaints on their part about what they perceived to be the irrelevance of theological education for their congregational missions. The most memorable expression of this antipathy was from a middle-aged pastor who was obviously seen by the others as a model to be emulated. He said this: "If I wanted to engage in study that would enrich my ministry, I would go to Harvard Business School long before I would choose a school like Fuller!"

Again, this kind of pragmatic approach to preparation for ministry is not new. Indeed, it has not been unique to issues of *theological* education. John Henry Newman devoted much of his classic *The Idea of a University* to a sustained critique of the notion, prevalent already in the nineteenth-century British context, "that no education is useful that does not teach some temporal calling, or some mechanical art, or some physical secret." Newman's book was a sustained critique of this pragmatic approach to higher education. Forming the "cultivated intellect," Newman famously argued, is "a good in itself"[1]

The lure of educational pragmatism has its own force, however, with reference to theological education, and nowhere in the Christian world is that force stronger than within the broad evangelical movement.

I. EVANGELICAL "PRACTICAL TRAINING"

Evangelical pragmatism regarding theological education is a many-faceted phenomenon. One factor is the strand of anti-intellectualism that has long been associated with classic pietism. Indeed, this strand has sometimes taken the shape of a rejection of formal theological training as such, as in this striking commentary by Peter Cartwright, a nineteenth-century circuit-riding preacher:

> Perhaps, among the thousands of traveling and local preachers employed and engaged in this glorious work of saving souls, and building up the Methodist Church, there were not fifty men that had anything more than a common English education, and scores of them not that; and not one of them was ever trained in a theological school or Biblical institute, and yet hundreds of them preached the Gospel with more success and had more seals to their ministry than all the sapient, downy D.D.'s in modern times, who, instead of entering the great and wide-spread harvest-field of souls, sickle in hand, are seeking presidencies or professorships in colleges, editorships, or any agencies that have a fat salary, and are trying to create newfangled institutions where good livings can be monopolized, while millions of poor, dying

sinners are thronging the way to hell without God, without Gospel.[2]

And even where the anti-intellectual spirit has not taken the form of a complete rejection of formal theological training, it has often been shaped by a conviction regarding the urgency of spreading the Gospel's influence. As the popular nineteenth-century hymn put it,

O Zion, haste, thy mission high fulfilling,
to tell to all the world that God is Light;
that he who made all nations is not willing
one soul should fail to know his love and might . . .
Behold how many thousands still are lying
bound in the darksome prison house of sin,
with none to tell them of the Savior's dying,
or of the life he died for them to win.

For many this sense of urgency has meant that Christians must often choose less than a full-orbed education for ministry. As F. W. Farr of the Nyack Missionary Training Institute put it in the 1880s, "It is best to know and to do, but it is better to do without knowing than to know without doing."[3]

Like Farr, A. J. Gordon, who founded Boston Missionary Training Institute in 1889, while firmly committed to providing the "knowing" element to persons engaging in various forms of Christian service, was explicit about keeping the formal learning aspect at a minimum, expressing the worry that "our Protestant ministry today . . . shall be impoverished by excess of learning." Gordon confessed that he was "perpetually chagrined to see how much better many of the unschooled lay preachers of our time can handle the Scriptures than many clergymen who have passed through the theological curriculum." In observing this, he explained, he did not mean to reject theological education as such. But it would be best, said Gordon, if "our teachers of theology were content to know less that they might know more, that they were less endued with the spirit of modern thought and more deeply baptized by that Spirit that has been sent to us 'that we might know the things that are freely given to us of God.'"[4]

The curricula of the Bible school movement held true, for almost a full century, to the emphasis on—to use Virginia Brereton's apt characterization—"brevity, practicality and efficiency."[5] These emphases profoundly shaped the ethos of the evangelical movement, and this influence was in some ways a gift to evangelicalism. One of the positive contributions, for example, was the education of thousands of women for leadership in (nonordained) ministry roles. A smattering of the older-style Bible schools still exist, but most of them—most notably, the ones founded by Farr, Gordon, and Dwight L. Moody, along with the Bible Institute of Los Angeles (BIOLA)—have become accredited seminaries characterized by a broad curriculum and solid teaching and scholarship.

The "practical training" emphasis that the Bible institute movement fostered during its heyday, however, has reappeared in recent years in congregations that are committed to a "grow our own" pattern of preparation for ministry, insisting on an exclusive on-the-job preparation for ministry. Some of these congregations are "megachurches" with capabilities to carry on ambitious programs of education in the Bible and ministry practices. Others associate with an "emergent" movement that characterizes itself in terms of various "posts": "postconservative," "postliberal," "post-Christendom"—and in this case, a "post" rejection of the ways in which all seminaries, evangelical and mainline, are much too beholden to the structures and contents of "modernity."

II. BUILDING RELATIONSHIPS

There was no inevitably about the evolution from the Bible institute to the full-fledged theological seminary. One can imagine cultural settings where the "practical training" school would continue to flourish as the primary mode of preparation for service in the church. It will not do, then, to insist that the local church mentoring model will eventually give way to the kind of education offered by seminaries.

While we must reject the inevitability thesis, then, there are still some historical factors that support a likely evolution from "grow our own" to an embrace of something like the traditional seminary model. I emphasize *something like* here because the seminary of the future will differ in significant ways from the seminary of the past and present.

I draw here on the example of theological education in my own Dutch Reformed tradition. In the early years of Protestantism's existence in the Netherlands, the Calvinist churches employed a mentoring model: candidates for ordination would work and study under the supervision of an older pastor in a local congregation. Soon, however, the responsibilities for this education came to be shared with other pastors in the region. A minister in one town might be more skilled in biblical languages and would accept responsibility for this mentoring with younger candidates from other congregations. This kind of curricular specialization soon spread. Finally, the distribution of labor led to establishing schools where full-time faculty took over the tasks.

In our present cultural context in North America, there are already factors at work that increase the pressure on local churches to look for more robust programs of theological education. An alumnus of Fuller Seminary once described to me the mentoring program within his own large congregation. He had benefited from his seminary education, he said, but he did not see it as a necessity for those moving toward church leadership under his own supervision. "Take my youth minister, for example," he said. "A graduate of a local junior college, quick learner, good relational skills. He is married with two kids. There is no way he is going to move his family to a seminary campus for a couple of years. And why should he? He is already good at what he does."

I did not argue the case, but I offered to be available if our seminary could ever be helpful to his ministry. Several months later, the alumnus called. Several members of the youth group were having extensive conversations about faith with Mormon friends at their high school. They were posing questions to the youth pastor that he could not respond to adequately. "It has to do with the attributes of God," the senior pastor said to me. "I remember studying that in a theology course at Fuller—it was about the 'communicable' and 'incommunicable' divine attributes. Could you find me a book on that for my youth pastor to read?" I did, and a few weeks later, the pastor called again. "That was so helpful to my youth pastor! Now he wants more. Are there some online theology courses he can take?"

That example points to a difference these days from the context in which an A. J. Gordon could recommend that church leaders "know less that they might know more." Church members—in this case, high school students—can bring questions to the church that often require some background in biblical, historical, and systematic understanding. In this example, the senior pastor, as a seminary graduate, had theological memories that informed his ability to guide his mentoree. We can hope that new modes of delivering theological education will be established in order to avoid a situation in which a new generation of mentors does not even know how to ask the questions about theological resources.

Theological educators in the evangelical world have to be persistent in making the case for theological education. We are not the only ones who need to take that challenge seriously these days, of course. "Alternative paths to ministry"—meaning options that bypass, in part or in whole, study in theological schools—are increasingly acceptable in many mainline denominations. A large part of the evangelical community, however, struggles with a long-standing bias against—or at least a fairly dominant pattern of suspicion of—theological education.

We cannot give in to the temptation, reinforced by our knowledge of how the Bible institute movement eventually got around to recognizing the strength of the traditional theological disciplines for ministry, simply to wait it out. Given the dramatic changes that have already taken place in theological education during the past two decades, a passive posture may mean losing what we still possess. The need to think new thoughts and build new relationships is urgent.

III. The *Sentire* Quest

As he came to the end of his active career in academia, Jaroslav Pelikan was asked to compare his time teaching at Valparaiso University with his later years on the faculty at Yale. Pelikan did not have kind thoughts about being on the faculty of a church-related academic institution. The best way to serve the Christian community, he said, is to work at a secular institution: "You have to give the church what it needs," he said, "not what it wants. And in order to do that you have to leave its payroll. It hurts me to say this because I want to be part of a church where that doesn't have to be said. But show me one where it is not true."[6]

In this brief comment, Pelikan was making much of the difference between being a theological scholar in the church's employ and pursuing one's theological calling in the secular academy. On this "payroll" issue, Pelikan was pointing to a genuine danger. A theological school must be free to be just that—a school that pursues theological inquiry in the context of the academy. This freedom can be greatly inhibited when theological teaching and scholarship is pursued under the direct scrutiny of church officials and members. But there are also dangers in maintaining too *much* distance between church and academy. Theological scholarship that falls completely within the domain of the academic guilds can often focus on topics and methods that are far removed from ministry contexts.

What is required is the kind of theological scholarship and teaching that engages in—to use a good Catholic phrase—*sentire cum ecclesia*. This phrase is sometimes translated as "thinking with the church," but *sentire* carries the sense of "feeling" as well. The thinking aspect must be expressive of an *empathy* for the church's life and mission. When pursued properly, this empathetic theologizing can occur by those on the church's payroll as well as those who serve other employers.

Here is a thought experiment I have posed to myself: What would it have been like for me to engage in some *sentire cum ecclesia* with the megachurch pastor who told me that he would prefer Harvard Business School to studying at a theological seminary?

For one thing, I would not simply have given up on him, resorting—as I did earlier—to using his declaration as an example of a belligerent antiseminary spirit. I had done much better in the case of the pastor who had gotten back to me about his youth pastor. In the latter situation, I had originally managed to communicate an understanding of the youth pastor's situation and encouraged further contact.

One of my fellow evangelical seminary presidents once asked a graduate of his school who is now in an "emerging church" kind of ministry how established seminaries could reach out to those of this pastor's colleagues who profess no interest in theological education. The pastor's reply: "Don't argue back with them. Give them some room later on to save face. Many of them will eventually recognize that they need more depth for sermon preparation and pastoral challenges. Don't make it too awkward for them to come to seminaries and ask for help!"

Back to the pastor enamored of Harvard Business School, then. What would it take to give him "room later on to save face"? One obvious step would have been for me to take his declaration as more than a rhetorical point. I could have asked him to help me understand why he thought that spending time hearing lectures on marketing, management, and the like would be more valuable for his ministry than in-depth study of the Bible and church history.

To be sure, he may not have been willing to go into that kind of detail with me, and he may have been too negative about theological education to ever get around to a "save face" position. But he and I were not the only ones in the room. There were some younger pastors witnessing our encounter who, while currently sympathetic with his outlook, may sense an openness to further conversations in the future.

Nor should showing an interest in the attraction to Harvard Business School be seen as a mere ploy to prepare the way for a "real" conversation. If theological education is to be seen by a new generation of Christian leaders, the theological schools must pay careful attention—expressive of a genuine commitment to *sentire*—to the concerns and questions that are actually on the minds of persons engaged in contemporary ministries.

IV. INTERESTS AND MEMORIES

The conversation with many of the pastors these days who express hostility to graduate theological education or question its value will rather quickly get around to another contrast posed in Pelikan's brief comment: "giv[ing] the church what it needs" as opposed to "what it wants." My own clear sense is that this way of putting things must itself be subject to serious critique.

A helpful way into this topic is provided by Stephen Ellingson's 2007 book *The Megachurch and the Mainline: Remaking Religious Tradition in the Twenty-First Century*—a study that deserves more attention than it has received thus far. In his book, Ellingson, a sociologist, provides in-depth accounts of the ways in which nine Lutheran congregations in the San Francisco area are responding to new challenges for the church's life and mission. While each of the congregations has its own unique character, Ellingson sees two very different patterns being explored. Borrowing terminology from the sociologist Robert Bellah and his *Habits of the Heart* coauthors, he sees some congregations attempting to be "communities of memory," while others are promoting a model associated with "communities of interest."[7]

The community of interest pattern is influenced by "megachurches," such as the Willow Creek and Saddleback congregations, where there is no longer any conscious intention to preserve a traditional denominational or confessional identity. The congregation's life and mission are designed to connect with the actual interests, the felt needs, of persons for whom that kind of traditional identity has no real meaning or attraction. Non-Christians who visit such a congregation will experience music, stories, and concepts that are much like what they experience in their surrounding culture. All this is a part of a deliberate strategy for encouraging the person to receive the Christian message in terms that are very familiar to them. It has become known as "seeker-sensitive worship," and it stands in contrast to a community of memory church where worship embodies confessional and denominational traditions that are not current in the larger culture.

Criticisms of the community of interest model have come from several sources. Denominational leaders, both mainline and evangelical, as well some younger advocates of "emerging church" themes, argue that the integrity of the Gospel requires that people who come to church be invited into an active worshiping community, one that takes seriously the teachings, practices, and symbols of the Christian tradition.

I have much sympathy for these criticisms. The worst of "seeker-sensitive" advocacy is exemplified by a report in a 1995 *New York Times* feature story on a major megachurch, where the reporter observed that the worship area "has no religious symbols, not even a cross on its façade." This is meant to convey the message "that religion is not a thing apart from daily life." And then he reinforces his observation by quoting one of the church's pastors as saying that on a recent visit to London's St. Paul's Cathedral, he found the building "not very user-friendly"—he was disappointed in both the lighting and the acoustics. His own church's architecture, the pastor observed, is clearly "more functional."[8]

I have kept that newspaper reference handy over the years to remind myself that there are indeed some genuine defects in the "seeker-sensitive" approach. But once again, it is tempting for many of us in theological education not to look beyond the bad aesthetics and superficial marketing jargon that often appears on the surface of the community of interest approach.

The need to probe more deeply is enhanced by the recognition that evangelicalism is itself a transdenominational, transconfessional movement that covers a broad spectrum of ecclesiologies.

The National Association of Evangelicals does not require its members to subscribe to a detailed ecclesiology. Nor does the Lausanne Covenant, generally seen as the closest the evangelical movement has come to a consensus "confessional" document, give any attention to the nature of the church. It should not surprise us, then, when a "generic" evangelicalism runs the risk of ecclesiological weakness.

If there is not careful attention, then, to ecclesiology within various evangelical subgroups, the resultant understanding of the church can be dangerously thin. A consensus evangelical theology is a weak basis for sustaining biblical orthodoxy. Much to be preferred is an evangelicalism that, sharing some fundamental convictions that are ignored and even explicitly denied in the larger Christian community, eagerly enters into a freewheeling discussion of what we can best draw upon from the "thick" confessional traditions of the past in addressing urgent questions today about the church's life and mission.

I am convinced that the argument for "thickness" needs to be heavily stressed in the present. Even where there is some attention to ecclesiological matters, the result is often a kind of bricolage project, with elements drawn from, say, the monastic tradition alongside some Anabaptist themes. Often, however, there is very little awareness at all historical explorations of the nature of the church.

Before saying more about the importance of ecclesiology for contemporary evangelicalism, however, I want to pursue a more positive theological path. In my own Reformed tradition, there are some good theological reasons for taking more seriously the emphasis on "seeker-sensitive" patterns in our church life. In fact, we can look even to John Calvin himself for positive encouragement on this subject. In his *Institutes*, Calvin focuses on two closely related theological themes for understanding the indelibly spiritual character of human existence, even in its fallen condition: the sense of divinity (*sensus divinitatis*) and the seed of religion (*semen religionis*).[9] All human beings, Calvin says, have a sense of the divine, whether they consciously acknowledge it or not. This is due to the fact that God has planted the seed of religion in every human heart. Human beings, even sinful human beings, yearn for God. As St. Augustine put it in the form of a prayer at the beginning of his *Confessions*, "Thou hast made us for thyself and our hearts are restless until they find rest in Thee."[10]

A more popular spiritual formulation of this same point is captured in the familiar Christmas carol line: "The hopes and fears of all the years are met in thee tonight." This is what both Augustine and Calvin are encouraging us to think about: the ways in which the basic hopes and fears of the human heart—even the sinful, as it may be—are in some way fulfilled in the redemptive ministry of Jesus Christ.

To be sure, our "natural" yearnings as sinners are fundamentally misdirected. Thus Calvin's graphic depiction: "The human heart is a factory of idols. Every one of us is, from his mother's womb, expert in inventing idols."[11] When, because of our sinful rebellion, we cut ourselves off from a vital relationship with our Creator, we seek to satisfy our hopes and calm our fears by putting our ultimate trust in something creaturely, in something that is less than the true God. But it is precisely because we are created for fellowship with the Living God that our idols never really satisfy our deepest yearnings. Our hearts are restless until they rest in the Living God.

Suppose, then, we ask the question that the sociologist Ellingson is posing in his book about megachurches and traditional churches: Should we attempt to be communities of interest or communities of memory? The Reformed answer, it seems to me, is that we must focus on both. The experienced "needs" of the unbelievers whom we want to reach with the Gospel are themselves expressions of deep, although certainly misdirected, yearnings that are planted by God in their hearts.

This does not mean, of course, that we simply take at face value the ways in which those persons describe their needs. We must identify the real nature of those needs by probing beneath the surface for the underlying God-implanted yearnings that give rise to what appears on the surface. There is an illustration that is regularly—but mistakenly—attributed to G. K. Chesterton that gets at this point in a provocative manner. It goes like this: the man who knocks on the door of a house of prostitution is looking for God.[12] Obviously the statement should not be taken as meaning that the man who approaches the house of prostitution hopes that God will be the one who greets him at the door. The real message is that people who are looking for ultimate fulfillment in the quest for sexual pleasure or wealth or power or any other element or aspect of creation will not find it in any of these things. The Westminster Shorter Catechism makes the point clearly: our chief end as human beings is to glorify God and to enjoy *God* forever. Nothing brings genuine fulfillment to the human spirit except an obedient relationship with our Creator.

V. HAVING THE CONVERSATION

I confess that I still have a difficult time imagining a productive conversation with the pastor who preferred a business school curriculum over a program in theological education. He is the kind of church leader who does not seem open to serious discussion with those of us in theological education. But many younger pastors who take their cues from leaders like him are more open. They have a genuine desire to find ways to be obedient to the Gospel in their ministries, and they are seeking effective ways to address the deepest hopes and fears of the human spirit. Discovering that the likes of St. Augustine and John Calvin, along with other thinkers of the Christian past, have addressed the topic of deeper yearnings can be the beginning of a longer conversation that can lead to making stronger connections between communities of interest and communities of memory.

And the truth is that those of us in theological education need to be genuine partners in those conversations. We have much to learn if we are to be effective in educating for the church's life and mission in our contemporary context. Our own efforts to be faithful educational communities of memory need to be enriched by a more profound engagement with those who have probed the actual "hopes and fears" of this present generation.

This kind of conversation with them will not be truly beneficial if we simply see it as leading to a point when they will finally listen to us seriously as we instruct them in traditional ways of thinking about the church's life and mission. Our efforts must be characterized by a genuine desire to be instructed by them, not only about how the yearnings of the human spirit get expressed in our contemporary context, but also about how this mutual quest can lead to new ways of configuring the life and mission of the church. The future of evangelical theological education is at stake in our willingness to engage in this new program of *sentire cum ecclesia*.

5

EVANGELICALS, MISSION, AND MULTIFAITH EDUCATION
Douglas McConnell

In my first year as a dean, I met a veteran missionary whose role in life seemed to be helping others enjoy witnessing to her faith in everyday encounters. She was an amazing example of the value of hospitality and a welcoming attitude. Since that first meeting fifteen years ago, my colleague Evelyne Reisacher continues to exemplify this approach to life in a multifaith world. Her recent book *Joyful Witness in the Muslim World: Sharing the Gospel in Everyday Encounters*[1] captures the essence of this gracious approach at the intersection of missiology, neuroscience, and Islamic studies.

The practice of joyful witness is foundational to the everyday encounters in a network of Muslim-born followers of Christ known as L'Ami based in France. The founder, Dr. Farida Saidi, a colleague of Reisacher, exemplifies this joyful encounter as a lifestyle and foundational philosophy of leadership. It was my privilege to work with Farida as she pursued her doctoral studies. Her focus was on the development of leaders with the understanding of religious and cultural influences while also cultivating significant skills that foster intercultural attachments.[2] I sat with Farida and a group of her colleagues in the L'Ami network while in South Africa. Our discussion centered on the pedagogical issues relating their approach to equipping lay leaders. Once again, I was impressed with the significance of their emphasis on joyful everyday encounters as essential to living together with people of other faiths.

Cultivating such a hospitable approach in a multifaith and multicultural world is an essential element in theological education. This was confirmed as an outcome of the two-year project titled the Christian Hospitality and Pastoral Practices in a Multifaith Society by the Association of Theological Schools (ATS). In his review of the project, Stephen Graham pointed to "the importance of training for pastoral practices in those contexts."[3] As a result, ATS revised the standard for MDiv degrees to "engage students with the global character of the church as well as ministry in the multifaith and multicultural context of contemporary society."[4] Based on the ATS project that led to the revision, the consensus is that focusing on hospitality and pastoral practices is core to implementing this standard.

Such an important revision must disseminate into the classrooms of theological educators working within their own theological and ecclesial traditions. It is there, as Dan Aleshire observes, that "faculty fulfill a priestly role by attending carefully to the changing situation in North American Christianity and North America's changing place in global Christianity."[5] As faculty our role requires equal attention to the high standards of theological education and to equipping people for the work of the church.[6] As theological educators, we share an important history of shaping Christian leaders from each of the traditions represented in ATS. The inherent challenges of setting and assessing standards that apply equally across such a wide spectrum of traditions are well illustrated by the revision to engage in multifaith contexts.[7]

In this essay, I explore the issues of implementing multifaith education from the perspective of an evangelical tradition steeped in a commitment to scholarship in theological education and world mission. As one would expect, the particularities of the evangelical movement influence curricular choices of how to engage the multifaith standard programmatically. The implementation of the revised standard by evangelicals engages the changing worlds and the unchanging mission of God with fresh insights from colleagues like Evelyne Reisacher and many others.

I. THE EVANGELICAL HERITAGE AND OUR MISSION MIND-SET

The evangelical tradition as used in ATS refers to schools that represent churches broadly grouped together from the evangelical movement. By way of disclaimer, it is difficult to speak authoritatively on behalf of evangelicals without noting that exceptions tend to be the rule. To illustrate, the word "evangelical" as used in contemporary political and social discourse has characteristics that do not uniformly represent the broad movement and indeed is questioned by many scholars and institutions.[8] I use the term to refer to the "quadrilateral of priorities" for evangelicals: the uniqueness of Christ and the crucifixion, the authority of the Bible, the need for changed lives through personal conversion, and activism that engages in the mission of God.[9] These four priorities are reflected in the statements of faith and curricular distinctives of evangelical institutions of ATS. They also govern the manner in which evangelicals approach participation in matters of accreditation.

During the consultations exploring multifaith and multicultural society, evangelicals raised several concerns over the terminology in line with these priorities. Stephen Graham summarized the issues: "The evangelicals noted that many within their family prefer to speak about *conversations* rather than *interreligious dialogue*. Other evangelicals recognize an existing *plurality* but resist *pluralism* which carries connotations of equality of religions. Similarly, *multifaith* is acceptable as a description of existing reality, whereas *interfaith* seems to presume a level of interaction that might not be appropriate from their perspective."[10]

Acknowledging our priorities and questioning the terminology raises the question, How does the revised standard of engaging the multifaith context impact evangelical institutions? Despite what may appear to be a desire to avoid the difficult issues, in fact just the opposite is true for evangelical institutions in ATS. Intrinsic to the quadrilateral of priorities is a mandate for global engagement emanating from a mission mind-set. The curricular emphasis is normally reflected structurally through departments, centers, or schools of world mission and intercultural studies—for example,

- Dallas Theological Seminary, Department of World Missions and Intercultural Studies
- Gordon Conwell Theological Seminary, J. Christy Wilson, Jr. Center for World Mission
- Southwestern Baptist Theological Seminary, World Missions Center
- Asbury Theological Seminary, E. Stanley Jones School of World Mission and Evangelism
- Biola University, Cook School of Intercultural Studies

The curricular approach growing out of our evangelical tradition is firmly based on the mission of God. Scott Sunquist, dean of Fuller Seminary's School of Intercultural Studies, provides an operational definition of mission that helps one understand the position.

> Christian mission is the church's participation in the Triune God through the suffering of Christ, who was sent by the Father for the redemption and liberation of the world by means of the conversion of individuals and cultures in the power of the Holy Spirit, to the end that God be glorified in the nations and in all his creation.[11]

The commitment to active engagement in the mission of God is a characteristic of evangelical institutions. Evangelicals tend to view the world with a mission mind-set based on the priority of activism evidenced in the emphasis given to extracurricular mission conferences and mission trips, both domestic and international. As seen in the structural commitment to missions, this activism is also embedded in the academic fabric of the institutions. The formal study of mission or missiology is an integrative approach to the study of the

Bible as the narrative of God's mission, the church that belongs to the mission, and the world of human beings and the cultures they create. The new reality is that the "world" has moved from overseas to next door, creating new opportunities for reflection and learning.

Missiology approaches the sending nature of God in a dynamic way, evaluating the methods and practices of mission in relation to the ever-changing contexts. Building on the historical and theological understanding of mission, missiology engages deeply with both the multifaith and multicultural contexts. Missiology as an eclectic study draws on scholarship from many Christian traditions and academic disciplines. An example is the inclusion of anthropological insights for mission. In 1953 Wheaton College anthropologist Robert Taylor launched a new journal titled *Practical Anthropology* to study languages and cultures relating to Christian and missionary practice. The journal merged with *Missiology*, a publication of the American Society of Missiology, in 1973 and continues to focus on understanding cultures and adapting our practices of intercultural engagement.[12]

Another significant focus of missiology is the engagement with people of other faiths. Terry Muck, dean emeritus of Asbury's School of World Mission, and Frances Adeney, professor of evangelism and global mission at Louisville Presbyterian Theological Seminary, provide an important study of Christian responsibility to people of other faiths. Their missiological approach to multifaith engagement explores the intercultural metaphor of gift giving, using the expression "giftive Mission."[13] From a biblical narrative of gift giving—grace, the incarnation, gifts of the Spirit—they explore the cultural and religious traditions of gift giving, establishing the significance of giftive mission in the context of relationships and hospitality. The giftive mission approach to other religions fits well with the joyful witness approach of Evelyne Reisacher.

Theological resources are also adding to our understanding of life in a multifaith world. Evangelical scholar Veli-Matti Kärkkäinen, building on his understanding of theology of religions and mission experience, has recently completed the five-volume series *A Constructive Christian Theology for the Pluralistic World*.[14] Theologian Amos

Yong, executive director of the Center of Missiological Research at Fuller Seminary, is moving evangelical reflection toward a more robust understanding of Trinitarian theology with particular insights into the work of the Holy Spirit.[15] Important works by evangelical ethicists with significant pedagogical implications are works by Richard Mouw, *Uncommon Decency: Christian Civility in an Uncivil World*, and Christine Pohl, *Making Room: Recovering Hospitality as a Christian Tradition*.[16] In each of these examples, the authors maintain a clear understanding of the evangelical priorities as they relate directly to the multifaith, multicultural contexts of ministry and mission.

Although mission as the framework for understanding the multifaith and multicultural worlds draws on a rich history of Christians engaging others, it also raises a critical concern that must be equally considered. At the heart of the evangelical tradition are priorities of the cross and conversion that form the substance of our witness. I was reminded of the depth of this conviction in a mission class last quarter. Together we reflected on the practices of witnessing and interfaith dialogue. A student serving as a missionary outside the US raised this tough issue: "I still struggle with the real purpose behind religious conversation. If I am truly and completely convinced that Jesus is the way, the truth, and the life, then I feel that I have an obligation both to God and the person to communicate that truth."[17] When one's convictions attest that salvation is found in no other name, then it must be part of the encounter.

II. Multifaith Engagement and the Mission Mind-Set

In 2010 it was my privilege to work with a group of scholars under the leadership of Lucinda Mosher and Justus Baird on a project sponsored by Auburn Seminary's Center for Multifaith Education and supported by a grant from the Wabash Center for Teaching and Learning in Theology and Religion. There were seven professors in the group representing multifaith education from Roman Catholic, mainline Protestant, and evangelical Protestant traditions as well as a Muslim faculty member from Hartford Seminary. Our task for the two-day gathering was to explore the pedagogical concerns surrounding the formation of religious leaders in the multifaith, multicultural world of North America. The insights we gained from our experience, readings, and discussions were invaluable for my own formation.[18] One of the most important insights was recognizing that each of us from our different traditions shared an abiding love for neighbors as a theological imperative.

One tangible outcome of our work together was the special issue of *Teaching Theology & Religion*.[19] Rabbi Justus Baird's article is a brief historical overview of the initiatives during the 2002–12 period identifying the issues arising out of the research and future questions facing theological educators. Baird observes that support for multifaith education primarily centers on demographics and theological factors. Our collective recognition of the rapidly changing demographic landscape is a reality that easily finds its way into our classrooms through the diverse participants as well as the rich literature available. Theological factors, on the other hand, tend to be more divided along the lines of our Christian traditions. Baird observes, "Seminary educators tend to embrace one of two lines of thought: (i) engaging in multifaith education enriches one's own faith; or (ii) in order to effectively proselytize, one must know something about other faiths."[20]

I had no problem recognizing the two lines of thought based on active participation during the decade, but as an evangelical educator, I experience both in the institutions with which I am familiar. My appreciation for the challenges was deepened by Baird's analysis of the surveys, reports, and gatherings. Of his nine additional observations, "1. Multifaith education tends to deepen, rather than dilute, religious commitment" and "9. Multifaith education forces a conversation about mission" most accurately address my own observations.[21] A pastoral student reflecting on the first observation posted, "The opportunity to be surprised . . . in and through the wrestling we will naturally engage in as our beliefs come into contact with others, is a beautiful byproduct of our willingness to respond to the commission we have been given in humble obedience."[22] This same deepening and enriching of one's faith is our experience after a decade of conversation with Mormons.[23]

The ninth observation that multifaith education confronts our view of mission is a central consideration in implementing the new standard. As Baird observed, many of us "would defend the right to engage in respectful mission work," adding "(including this author)."[24] Evangelicals readily identify with this general observation, and I personally appreciate Baird's affirmation as an example of his convictions. For evangelicals the integration of faith and culture is located in the classic exclusivist position to other religions in harmony with the priority of the crucifixion of Christ. It is a matter of fidelity deep in the heart of the faith tradition. In the words of Baptist pastor Edward Mote, so often sung in evangelical churches, "On Christ the solid rock I stand, all other ground is sinking sand."[25] The result as articulated by the missionary student post is that we still struggle with the real purpose of multifaith engagement.

III. LEARNING FROM OTHERS: AN EVANGELICAL CASE STUDY

A helpful way to frame the educational dilemma is Baird's follow-up question: "But what does respectful evangelism look and feel like?"[26] Beginning with the conviction that mission is a mandate based on an evangelical understanding of the Great Commission, the issue is one of civility. This approach builds on the concept of convicted civility from *Uncommon Decency* by Richard Mouw.[27] Helping students understand how to communicate their deep convictions begins by reviewing the beliefs and histories that sustain the tradition. In seminary education, the source of these convictions normally develops through courses in biblical studies, theology, history, and context-specific inquiry, whether practical or cultural. Implementing the engagement with the diversity of religious traditions requires opportunities, both curricular and extracurricular, to understand one's own convictions and how to respond with civility. It is not commonly achieved in any single course in the program, so educators must consider how and where the integration of the various streams of learning become convictions rather than subject matter from coursework.

Curricular changes at Fuller Seminary illustrate a particular response to integration for convicted civility. In master's-level theology and missiology degrees, all students are required to complete four integrative courses that build on twenty-eight Christian practices organized around vocation and formation, worship, community, and mission. Each of the courses combines academic reflection through reading, lectures, and discussions to identify and form integrated convictions around these four common elements. Critical to this pedagogy is moving from content to reflection on the practices. The four integrative courses also include vocational formation (VF) groups led by practitioners, most of whom are Fuller alumni. The VF groups focus on personal, spiritual, academic, and global formation. This formational approach is proving to be an important means of achieving the standard of engaging the global character of the church through practices such as hospitality, friendship, witness, advocacy, and interfaith dialogue. In these settings, convicted civility is facilitated in the context of relationships both within the VF group and in diverse religious communities.

By focusing on vocational formation as foundational, more traditional courses develop the ability to think theologically and missiologically in the context of the practices. The skills of civility are thereby integrated with the convictions intrinsic to theological education. An important element of this curricular approach is the assessment of learning outcomes as they align in the programs and degrees. Parallel to the implementation of the courses on Christian practices and VF groups is a robust assessment schedule to ensure the integration is more than a curricular hope. A group of faculty and administrative leaders assess the student feedback against the outcomes for each course regularly, making incremental adjustments. Regular interaction with faculty, building on the required prerequisite training courses, has proven to be a vital element of quality control. These major changes to the curriculum were implemented in 2013, the year after the revised standard for multifaith and multicultural engagement.

We are currently teaching the course used as a reference point for my article on multifaith theological education in 2013.[28] A noticeable improvement over the years is our students' understanding of convicted civility in the context of multifaith and multicultural society today. This was evident in the first discussion assignment this quarter asking if it is more important to emphasize civility or your convictions. Representative of the seventeen student responses is this comment: "I have a duty to speak the truth to my neighbor. Additionally, I believe that I should not force someone to accept my faith as their own. Thus, convicted civility is the only way forward. I emphasize civility over conviction in practice by establishing relationships before creating tension or friction through personal convictions. This connects with a vision of hospitality that makes room for the other in my life, heart, and mind."[29]

IV. ENGAGED EXCLUSIVISM AND MISSION

An important shift is taking place in the evangelical tradition of theological education, a move toward engaging with diverse religious traditions that goes beyond the quadrilateral of priorities that frame an exclusivist position. Timothy Tennent, missiologist and president of Asbury Theological Seminary, has recognized the growing trend toward an "engaged exclusivist" understanding that "maintains optimism regarding God's preparatory activity through general revelation and the necessity of maintaining a missiological focus in all evangelical theologizing."[30] His use of the term *engaged exclusivist* resonates with many in the evangelical tradition as a way of expressing the heart of convicted civility. As our student noted, speaking the truth and hospitality are both required.

For evangelicals, recognizing God's providential activity in the world has serious implications. Allen Yeh makes a strong case for the new realities of mission "from everyone to everywhere" as truly global Christianity.[31] This polycentric mission takes place across the globe, removing the once strongly held "West to the rest" perspective. An important implication is that evangelicals must engage in every situation and every context as part of God's preparatory activity. As Yeh suggests, Christianity has no majority ethnic group and "no geographical center."[32] The diversity of religious traditions as an intrinsic part of every context means that the mission of God, as evangelicals understand it, compels them to maintain optimism and a missiological focus. Thankfully, there is an increasing awareness that the best way to put this into practice is joyful witness in the multifaith world.

The escalation of transmigration is redefining the religious as well as cultural landscape. As theological educators, we recognize this as the new norm, prompting the revision of standard number A.2.3.2 to include multifaith and multicultural context. In ATS the variety of perspectives and motivations converge from across a continuum of pluralist, inclusivist, and exclusivist understandings. The goal is to hold one another accountable within our diverse traditions as peer institutions in theological education. The evangelical tradition, not unlike the Catholic and mainline traditions, is adapting to the changing world in ways that must be responsive. It behooves us as evangelicals to teach the knowledge and skills necessary to engage with convicted civility.

Justus Baird raised eight important future questions in his review of multifaith education. Each question is worthy of further reflection with our faculty colleagues if we are to maintain our identities while also engaging the multifaith world. From my perspective, the question that draws an immediate answer based on the case study of Fuller Seminary is number 7, "Should multifaith education goals be framed as content or competencies? Should it be delivered through defined courses, across the curriculum, or through the institution's setting and supplemental programs?"[33]

With all conviction and civility, the answer is YES!

6

WHAT ABOUT OTHER RELIGIONS?
Opportunities and Challenges in
Mainline Theological Education
Judith A. Berling

I. An Increasingly Interreligious America

Up until the middle of the twentieth century, the prevailing view was that the United States was a Christian country with a small but important presence of Jews. In 1955 Will Herberg published *Protestant, Catholic, Jew: An Essay in American Religious Sociology*.[1] The United States was more religiously diverse than Herberg depicted, even then, but the perception was that these three religions "defined" the American religious field. In elementary school in the 1950s, I was taught that the other religions were "located" elsewhere, shown on color-coded maps.[2] All that changed gradually after the 1965 Immigration and Naturalization Act opened doors to migrants from Asia and the Pacific, who brought with them their cultures, cuisines, and religions. Other immigrants came from the Caribbean, Central and South America, the Middle East, and Eastern Europe. The cultural and religious mix has intensified steadily over the past five decades. Diana Eck has vividly traced the impact of this increasing religious pluralism in her important book *A New*

Religious America: How a "Christian Country" Has Become the World's Most Religiously Diverse Nation.[3]

As the cultural and religious demographics of the country changed, the new situation began to affect the religious lives of Americans, including Christians. A vibrant "marketplace" of religious ideas and practices developed, with a rich plethora of books; classes in yoga, meditation, and the martial arts; shamanic healers; Hindu and Buddhist temples; Sikh Gurdwaras; and Neo/Pagan communities and centers. Persons from Christian households rubbed shoulders with adherents of other religions in schools, hospitals, workplaces, and marketplaces. Soon many Christian families included members (by birth or marriage) who had practiced another religion for a period, or who were exploring another religion, or who were seriously committed to observing another religion. Religious intermarriages became increasingly common, and children from Christian households were exploring or even committing to other religions.

These examples of religious mixing or experimentation raised issues in parishes. Was it acceptable for Methodist women in southern Illinois to be taking classes in Hatha Yoga? How were Christian parents to handle the religious explorations of their children? Ten years ago, my parish asked me to be a Confirmation Companion to a young woman who was exploring both Buddhism and Christianity. How were pastors to counsel Christians in interfaith marriages when both spouses wished to honor their religious traditions? How were pastors to honor the experience of East Asian Christian migrants, whose families were still deeply Confucian and/or Buddhist? Some of these persons experienced themselves as a sort of hybrid—intrapersonally interreligious. Were Christians or Christian pastors called to be engaged in interreligious dialogue, interfaith councils, or interreligious service in their communities? How should Christians respond to anti-Semitism, Islamophobia, attacks on Hindus or Sikhs, or other examples of religiously based intolerance in their communities? After World War II, with its grim experience of the Holocaust, some Christians felt the need to dialogue with and reach out to Jews to combat anti-Semitic strains in "Christian culture," but the world is now even more complex. How would pastors be prepared to teach, counsel, lead, and guide Christians in this complex world?

II. EARLY RESPONSES

In 2013 the journal *Teaching Theology & Religion* published a special volume on multifaith theological education.[4] The first article in the issue is Justus Baird's very helpful history of the development of multifaith education in seminaries and theological schools, particularly from 2002 forward.[5] As early as the 1980s and 1990s, Christian-Jewish education was initiated at Hartford Seminary and the Graduate Theological Union, and Andover-Newton Theological School developed a partnership with Hebrew College in Boston.[6] But particularly from 2008 on, there was an "explosion" of multifaith programs, funded in large part by the Henry Luce Foundation.[7] Those programs and a number of leaders in the field of multifaith education were represented in the special issue of *Teaching Theology & Religion*.

In 2009 Eboo Patel founded the Interfaith Youth Core (IFYC), whose primary mission is development of "civic interfaith leaders in a religiously diverse democracy."[8] While IFYC primarily focuses on developing community leaders, they have done workshops in and for a number of schools and developed curriculum suggestions for doing interfaith education. Some theological/divinity schools have benefited from IFYC programs. The distinctive approach of IFYC is well captured in Eboo Patel's *Interfaith Leadership: A Primer.*[9]

The American Academy of Religion, the Council for the Parliament of the World's Religions' 2009 meeting, Auburn Seminary, and the Association of Theological Schools have all established programs for faculty and/or seminarians to develop expertise in this field. The Association of Theological Schools ran a two-year project from 2010 to 2012 called Christian Hospitality and Pastoral Practices in a Multifaith Society. The project provided small grants to eighteen schools to facilitate engagement with the lived faith of religious communities and develop their school's work in this area.[10] The fruits of several of these grants were published in the special issue of *Teaching Theology & Religion*, cited earlier. And the project led to a new Association of Theological Schools (ATS) Accreditation Standard A.2.3.2 for MDiv programs: "M.Div. education shall engage students with the global character of the church as well as ministry in the multifaith and multicultural context of contemporary society. This should include attention to the wide diversity of religious traditions present in potential ministry settings, as well as expressions of social justice congruent with the institution's mission and purpose."[11] This interest and support have led to some excellent experiments and programs, but theological schools have only begun to address this issue. Justus Baird ended his article in 2013 with these words: "Yet it is incumbent upon theological educators to form communities of learning and practice to further the field. Engaging and learning about other faiths is an inherently boundary-crossing activity. There is much to learn from each other about *how* to learn about each other."[12]

III. OPPORTUNITIES

The good news is that we are starting to form communities of learning and practice, to exchange ideas and strategies, and to learn from one another's experiences. As Daniel Aleshire retired in 2017, there were promising developments among those committed to interreligious learning. The American Academy of Religion, the broadest guild of religious and theological scholars, has a unit on interfaith/interreligious studies that provides both visibility and a platform for the development of ideas among the range of religious studies and theological scholars. Additional professional associations are being created in the US and Europe, and there are journals devoted to the field, including *Journal of Interreligious Studies* and *Interreligious Studies and Intercultural Theology*. Through these organizations and through foundation initiatives, leaders in the field are writing volumes to share best practices and critical reflections and are sponsoring a range of workshops and seminars to educate faculty and theological leaders about how to design and adapt interreligious learning for their institutions. Eboo Patel and his Interfaith Youth Core are also active in training institutions and leaders in their approach to interreligious learning. The Pluralism Project at Harvard University has developed interreligious case studies, based on careful ethnographic research, to be used as teaching tools. These complex cases challenge students to engage deeply in interreligious analysis and to consider how to engage across religious borders.[13]

A number of institutions have taken advantage of the religious pluralism in our society to develop courses and programs that have not only interreligious goals but an intentionally interreligious student body or learning community. Andover Newton's Circle Program, originally begun informally by students, was institutionalized to pair students from the Christian seminary and Hebrew Union College as learning pairs with a strong commitment to learning from and with each other.[14] The Graduate Theological Union in Berkeley now includes an Institute for Buddhist Studies, Center for Jewish Studies, Center for Islamic Studies, and Center for Dharma Studies. The faculty and students from these varied traditions come together to offer intentionally interreligious courses with students from Christian and many other traditions. Emblematic, perhaps, is the annual Madrassa-Midrasha course, which brings together Muslim and Jewish faculty and Jewish, Muslim, and Christian students, using Muslim and Jewish texts and pedagogies, to engage a common issue.[15] Even in the midnineties, Mary Boys, a Roman Catholic from Union Theological Seminary, and Sara Lee of Jewish Theological Seminary used a Lilly Endowment grant to establish a course in which roughly equal numbers of Christian and Jewish students studied together and debated issues from their two traditions.[16]

Chicago Theological Seminary hired a Jewish faculty member to teach Jewish-Christian courses, but the institution soon decided that it needed intentionally to recruit Jewish students to create a genuinely interreligious experience.[17] Many schools have determined that interfaith education is not learning *about* another religion but learning *from and with persons* from other religions.[18] This need for actual relationships with persons from other religions is sometimes addressed by recruiting discussion partners or making extensive site visits, but some have found that the best model is an intentionally interreligious classroom.

The increase of religious diversity in the society creates opportunities for theological students to visit the sites (temples, gurdwaras, synagogues, etc.) of other religions. This is an excellent opportunity so long as the school lays the groundwork both with those institutions (to see whether and under what circumstances a visit is appropriate) and with their students so that they know how to behave courteously and appropriately in the new environment. Also, it is very possible to find speakers and resources from other traditions; there are ample opportunities to move beyond a textbook to a live engagement with the religions. Granted, the availability of sites or representatives of other religions varies from location to location. If such access is limited, it is important to choose films or books that represent authentic (and preferably multiple) voices of the tradition.[19]

IV. Challenges

Despite the rich resources and opportunities to engage with other religions, there are many challenges for theological institutions wishing to go down this path.

The most fundamental challenge, even if resources from other religions are readily available, is how to integrate interfaith learning into theological education. Simple exposure to another religion (a site visit, a dialogue, an immersion trip, a weekend program, etc.) is simply an "add-on" experience if it is not integrated into the rest of the educational experience. Given the school's understanding of theological education and religious formation or leadership, what is the purpose of the interfaith experience? What are the students to take away from the experience? If such experiences are part of a course, the school/instructor needs to articulate clear goals and learning outcomes, with appropriate analysis or reflection on the part of the student or the class in conversation to demonstrate those outcomes. In other words, if a crucial aspect of interfaith learning is to be exposed to or enter another religious space or practice or to establish a relationship with someone from another religion, how is that learning experience to be reintegrated into the student's educational goals—especially the theological dimension of those goals—if he or she is a theological student? Mere exposure may "broaden" students' experiences, but how does it enrich their understanding of their Christian faith or identity or of their role as religious leaders or teachers?

In my book *Understanding Other Religious Worlds*, I stress that the conversational and dialogical aspect of interreligious learning moves back and forth between being challenged by or opened to a very different religious understanding and responding from one's own location, entering another religious world, and coming back to reflect on what is learned. Then ultimately this understanding must be "lived" in new relationships or in a nuanced sense of one's own religious role or identity.[20]

Since each theological school has its own distinctive denominational identity and mission, the task of integrating interreligious learning will vary from school to school. Some schools will have the goal of their students establishing relationships of understanding with persons from other religions, as they will engage such persons either in their congregations or in the communities where they will serve. Others will focus on developing skills of Christian theological reflection on how a Christian engages another religion. For instance, in an evangelical school, a course on World Religions in Christian Perspective might have as the major focus theology of religions—that is, Christian theological reflection on other religions.[21] Theological schools are still exploring how interreligious education contributes to their missions as theological schools. This reflection on the reason for interreligious education is critical, for without clear understanding of the purpose of interreligious education, schools cannot structure learning experiences that will genuinely enhance their students' programs.

There is a host of practical challenges to successful interreligious education in theological institutions. One is the economic stress on theological schools, especially mainline theological schools. The outstanding Circle Program, which was a collaboration between Andover Newton and Hebrew Union College, has come to an end because Andover Newton, under financial strain, moved to become associated with Yale Divinity School. Some schools reaching out to Muslim communities are encountering "ambassador fatigue" among communities that are called upon again and again to help "others" understand them.[22] Such fatigue can also arise if a school relies on sending students to visit a temple or religious site again and again. Maintaining appropriate relationships with "minority" religious communities who serve as resources is a delicate matter requiring sensitivity and empathy. Christians seeking relations with "minority" religions need to ask ourselves what they have to offer the "other" religions and what benefit their non-Christian partners might gain from the relationship.

Schools of all types are facing enrollment stresses. The numbers of members in mainline denominations are in decline, meaning less demand for ordained leadership and a smaller student pool. The number of Roman Catholic seminary students is small. Evangelical schools function in a world where the need for seminary education is often questioned. The difficulties in recruiting students are exacerbated by the economic challenges of students facing high tuition costs and large student loans, with limited promise of employment and adequate salary. Fewer students means less revenue for institutions that depend on tuition—even endowed institutions that do not make cuts as student numbers increase. This has led to fewer full-time faculty, fewer on-campus courses, and thus fewer electives and "enrichment" courses. Schools are cutting back to the basics—core courses in the "classical" and practical disciplines. While this is an understandable response to severe institutional stress, it has led to the end of very successful courses. Luther Seminary in Saint Paul, for example, had an outstanding course taught in the community in Lutheran churches located in neighborhoods that now have large

Muslim populations. The course helped students and parish leaders understand the neighborhoods better and explore how and in what ways they could better understand, engage with, and serve the interreligious community, including the Muslim neighbors. The students benefited from hands-on engagement in ministry in the new demographic environment of the Twin Cities. Although the course was very successful and highly evaluated,[23] it was made an every-other-year elective because it wasn't "core" to the Lutheran ordination requirements.[24] The financial and enrollment strains on theological schools and dwindling numbers of full-time faculty are a genuine obstacle to envisioning new approaches to theological education.

V. A Central Conceptual Challenge

Some fifteen years ago at a faculty consultation at Auburn Seminary, one of the participants declared that the mainline denominations were like dinosaurs: they were extinct but did not realize it yet. He meant it as a provocation—even a joke—but there is more than a grain of truth in his statement. Sociologist Robert Wuthnow has been analyzing the decline of denominations as a critical factor in the religious identity of Americans; most are more likely to choose a church with the sorts of programs and services they desire than because of denominational affiliation.[25] He and other sociologists have also noted the rise of "community" or "nondenominational" churches. This is not good news for those in denominational theological schools. Roman Catholic schools are facing a steep decline in priestly vocations, significant demographic shifts in the makeup of congregations, and challenges in response to years of sexual scandals. More recently, even evangelicals who appeared to be booming are beginning to experience attrition in numbers.

Beyond the general decline of denominationalism is the rise of the "nones," the "spiritual but not religious." The "nones" are the fastest growing religious affiliation in the US, and they are beginning to appear in theological schools, bringing a general interest in spiritual issues but no religious affiliation. I vividly remember the time a "none" appeared in my class about Confucianism and Christianity. The overwhelming majority of the students were Roman Catholics of Asian ancestry, but a very bright student who was steeped in Hindu traditions (he knew Sanskrit quite well) absolutely refused to claim any religious affiliation. This was, unsurprisingly, very difficult for Asian Catholics to wrap their minds around, and he could not grasp their strong commitment to a clear religious identity. It made for fascinating, if often unresolved, conversations.

The combination of challenges from changes and/or declines in church affiliations and the rise of the "nones" poses a difficult challenge for theological schools: their missions are centered on perpetuating their traditions through theological scholarship and the formation of leaders, and yet denominational/church teachings and identity are less and less important in our culture. The matter is, of course, complex, for while Americans may choose a church based on, say, its youth programs rather than its affiliation, once they join, they often want to learn more about the church's tradition. Having chosen a parish, they now want to understand the theological and liturgical implications of that choice. And based on my personal experience, the rise of the "nones" has also created a reaction in other millennials and young people, who react by wanting a clear religious identity, a clear location among the marketplace of choices. And to be sure, it is difficult to train for ordination in a particular church without some clear sense of its tradition and identity. Those of us who have chosen theological education as our vocation are naturally deeply engaged with our tradition. It is not, then, a matter of rejecting tradition but of discerning how best to teach tradition as well as an effective understanding of and openness to the complex interreligious and intercultural US religious environment.

Issues of church identity and tradition are all too easily subsumed by institutional and economic worries about the future of the church organization, the churches, and the theological school itself. In our era, dominated by corporate mind-sets, we are consumed with the issues of "the brand" and "finding our niche." But it can be helpful to step back and think about tradition from a number of perspectives not tied to institutional identity.

First, serious students of history are well aware that "Christianity" and its various traditions have always arisen from and existed in religiously plural environments, interacting with other religious options, contending with them, and adapting items liberally from the pool of religious practices, ideas, and symbols. The narrative we tell about the origins and development of traditions is often a radical simplification, suggesting a tradition developing in splendid isolation, following its own internal logic. That narrative can lift up what the leaders of a community at a specific time and place thought was central and important to their religious vision, but it obscures the circumstances in which the community took shape. For instance, Cynthia Bourgeault, in *The Wisdom Jesus*, points out that "the Silk Road went right through the city of Capernaum, where Jesus did a lot of his learning and teaching. It was an environment in which he would have been fully exposed to a variety of ideas that could be seen as the New Age of his time."[26] Traditional Biblical scholarship has taught us a great deal about various religious developments in Jewish and local cultures of Jesus's time, but the fact that Jesus was learning and teaching along the Silk Road opens a much broader horizon of religious ideas and symbols that may have inspired or influenced the development of the early Christian community.

Second, social historians and anthropologists have made us aware that "tradition," as commonly taught in theological schools (Bible, theology, ethics, or church teachings), is the "tradition" that is in the hands of (overwhelmingly) male and elite church leaders and is not synonymous with the religious beliefs and practices of "ordinary" Christians. William Christian, in his book *Local Religion in Sixteenth-Century Spain*,[27] illustrated how the beliefs and practices of villagers were quite different from the "orthodox" teachings and practices promulgated by church authorities. Robert Orsi wrote a fascinating ethnographic study of the religious beliefs and practices of his Italian family members and of Cuban Americans in Florida, documenting how their beliefs in and veneration of the saints strongly resisted the changes of Vatican II. These faithful were following their own beliefs and defying religious authorities to do so.[28]

Context can also have an important impact on "tradition," particularly in the global church. Richard Madsen has noted that Roman Catholicism in some parts of rural China is characterized by practices and rituals that look more like millenarian Buddhism than Western Roman Catholicism. Their need to rely on local priests and bishops (because the PRC government does not allow for Roman appointments of Chinese Catholic officers) and limited education in traditional Catholic teachings and practices (there are no parochial schools) has meant that the religious patterns and mores of these Catholics draw more heavily on patterns shaped by earlier Buddhist traditions than by "standard" (i.e., Western) Catholic practices. Thus while the faith of Christian converts in parts of rural China may be fervent, their version of Christian tradition might look very unfamiliar to a Western Christian.[29]

Moreover, those who have studied the history of Christian theology recognized that "tradition" is always contested. Each generation (re)interprets tradition to make it "speak to" their age and their issues. They not only adapt present teachings to the present age but also reframe or revise the historical narrative of the tradition to support their current understanding. Tradition is not and never has been settled for all time, though each denomination and group have some historical documents or principles that must be honored and invoked to support present understandings.

The teaching of "tradition" has also been nuanced by the rise of feminist, contextual, liberationist, queer, and body theologies, which insist that theological reflection begins from a specific embodied (and often complex) location, an intersection of "identities" and experiences. Rather than trying to fit human experience into "traditional" church doctrine, these theological approaches bring experience and social location to bear on church doctrine, dialoguing with it, interrogating it, and often critiquing it.

We have long been aware of the issues I have discussed here, but how many schools have thought deeply about how these "complications" of tradition impact (or should impact) our approach to other religions and "nones" in theological education? In my experience, we all too often approach "others" (representatives of other religions or "nones") as though we have a clear and distinct tradition and they do (or should) as well. When we "default" to that assumption of a clear and bounded tradition, we miss opportunities for interreligious learning.

First, if we remember that our "traditions" have always existed in interaction with other "traditions," we will recognize that Christians and all people have always encountered, learned from, or absorbed ideas, practices, or images from religious others. We unconsciously tend to construct "interreligious encounters" as new and fraught with challenges, whereas humans of all faiths have always noticed and responded to "other religions." My favorite example of this was a story told to me by a devout Portuguese Catholic friend, who—though she lives in San Francisco—maintained ties with a Portuguese Catholic community in a town about an hour north. She would especially visit on feast days, when the Portuguese Catholic church members would process with their patron saint through the streets of the town. They were joined one year by a group of Japanese Buddhists, who were drawn to the familiar practice of processing with the image of a "saint," for it was their practice to process with an image of the Buddha on their special festivals. The two groups began attending each other's festivals, developing a mutual relationship based on a similar practice.

Second, if we remember that any person's "tradition" has been profoundly shaped by context and complex intersectional social locations, we will pull back from expecting our seminarians or those whom they meet to represent "the" tradition. Each person will be a specific incarnation or embodiment of his or her tradition/s. Interreligious learning is more about relationships with specific persons than engaging "entire" traditions. The learners are encountering specific stories, persons, examples who incarnate specific aspects of traditions, just as in our social relationships, we gradually develop more complex and nuanced understandings of the complexities of human variety. Remembering this removes the onus on a person to "represent" an entire tradition, too large a burden for anyone.

Third, the principle of particular embodiment of tradition may help us to understand the "nones" more deeply. I have seen (and have myself earlier fallen into) a tendency to dismiss the "nones" as having a consumerist, "cafeteria" approach to religion—picking up tidbits here and there in a rather superficial sampling. While there is certainly a lively marketplace of religious goods (books, classes, remedies, healers, events, etc.), it is problematic to assume that the "spiritual but not religious" is a superficial consumerist movement. As a scholar of religion, I admit to a profound bias that knowledge about the sources, context, and background of a text or practice profoundly enriches one's understanding and experience of it and that participation in a community of interpretation connects one to the dynamic of a living tradition. However, the "nones" whom I have encountered in my teaching (granted, they are a subset with enough interest in religion to seek out a theological school) often have considerable knowledge of one or more traditions—even of their classical languages—but they resist declaring an affiliation or commitment. I have learned to respect that on two different levels. First, as a scholar of Chinese religions with more knowledge of and facility with Chinese sacred texts than some native adherents, I have been profoundly enriched (the Indians might say "spiced") by my study of these traditions. But precisely because I understand how committed thinkers and practitioners have deeply practiced, engaged, and struggled with those traditions, I would never claim to "be" a Confucian or a Daoist. Second, at least since the middle of the twentieth century, many have felt increasing dis-ease with institutional religions. There are issues of historical complicity of institutional religions in disasters like the Holocaust, resistance of institutional religion to forms of modernization or societal reform, implications of religion in colonialism and many forms of violence, and the decline of religion as a force shaping the culture and society in Europe and North America.

While the secularization thesis of mid-twentieth-century sociologists has proved to be mistaken, there has been a cultural move either beyond or to a very different relation to "institutionalized" religion. Since the middle of the twentieth century, for instance, the development of modern art (especially abstract expressionism) has given rise to a number of influential artists who were deeply spiritual, by their own accounts, but who eschewed clear identification with a specific religion. They were trying to grasp or express a spiritual dimension beyond or within forms without being tied to any single tradition. I am thinking of artists like Rothko, Kandinsky, Agnes Martin, and Andy Goldsworthy.[30] This "spiritual but not religious" impetus has been an influential strand in our culture for more than fifty years. And though I am a committed Episcopalian, I find myself profoundly drawn to the work of these artists. This suggests that even many of us who identify clearly with a specific religious denomination also swim in the pervasive "cultural soup" of the spiritual but not religious because the culture we engage (art, film, literature, theater, etc.) often explores or expresses this spirituality not located within any particular tradition.

Educating students in a particular tradition while simultaneously avoiding the notion of a tightly bound, neat, isolated tradition and being open to engagements with other religions or with "nones" may seem impossible and paradoxical, but it is so only to the extent that we hold to the habit of categorizing people into tidy religious boxes. A student-centered contextual pedagogy will challenge tidy categorizations. The principles discussed earlier call for a form of student-centered pedagogy, beginning from students' complex intersectional locations. If we allow students to bring their complex backgrounds and stories into the learning environment, they will model to each other (and, surprisingly, also to themselves) how complex "religious identity" is in this diverse world. Teachers need to honor students' stories about their religiously diverse environments, families, and lives, seeing that diversity as in no way exceptional in a religiously diverse and global world. Members of the learning community should share their complex, often hybrid identities (religiously and otherwise) as a way of being in the world, learning that they will no doubt meet many other people with similarly complex locations (even if the "mix" of the complex identities is different). And finally, students need to learn about themselves and others that their complex intersectional stories, while all authentic stories, are particular embodiments of various traditions, ethnicities, and so on: each person's life experiences give his or her story (of religion and much else) authenticity, but (as noted earlier) no one person's experiences represent the entirety of a tradition or an ethnic group or a culture or a gender. None of us need carry the burden of representing an entire culture or group or religion. Long ago, Wilfred Cantwell Smith reminded us that every adherent of a tradition has a particular and limited experience of the broader tradition of which she is a part—no one, not the founder nor the current leader of a tradition, embodies the full variety of that tradition as it has been experienced by many persons in many times and places.[31]

Many theological classrooms honor students' locations and experiences. If we can do so with some critical attention to how that pedagogical approach "loosens" the notion of tradition and opens it to other religions and spiritualities not bound by traditions, theological teachers and learners will begin to hold "tradition" more flexibly and openly. Perhaps because we are worried about the decline of the denominations or of churches, we can all too easily fall into the trap of seeing the flexible or "loose" hold of tradition as a threat. I believe that we (and I put myself first in this line) must instead use this classroom experience of flexibility and loosening as a chance for continuing and probing theological reflection on where and how God/Love/the Gospel appears in this flexible and open relationship of Christians to the broader culture and the world.

I have argued earlier that interreligious learning is not important because it is a "nice" thing to do, nor even because of the mere fact of religious diversity. Interreligious learning is important because Christian lives and Christian ministry now exist in close engagement with religious "others" in families, workplaces, society, and even—increasingly—within the lives of individual Christians. Religious diversity and the cultural pervasiveness of the "spiritual but not religious" elements that transcend any single tradition are the context within contemporary Christianity resides and—I am convinced—the context in which Christians must deeply discern and reimagine the Christian message and values. Christianity is an incarnational religion; we believe that God with Us has taken human form to embody God's saving love in the world. As the world evolves and changes, we as theological educators need to help students open their hearts, minds, and faith to discern the incarnation of God's love and presence in our day. They in turn will help lead Christians and others to perceive and respond to that presence.

AFTERWORD
Daniel O. Aleshire

Theological schools are about ideas, big ideas that begin with the love and grace of God, continue with the goodness and justice of God, and end with hope in the mercy of God. These ideas shape and mold; they bring revelation to minds and tears to hearts. They give meaning to life and evoke action in the world.

Ideas find their expression in words—sounds that can be gentle or dramatic, text that can compound meaning or magnify precision. Theological schools attend carefully to words that have been said or written and exert huge energy in creating more words to continue a tradition and fit old understandings to changing intellectual moments.

In the Christian tradition, the words can become flesh. This began with the Word that was in the beginning and continues with people who practice what they preach, who have been so formed by faith that its ideas are rooted in them like the muscle learning in a pianist's fingers. They are people who do the loving thing, or the faithful thing, or the moral thing by habit more than by calculation. Words in flesh are the most compelling of words.

The essays in this volume are thoughtful words that explore ideas central to understanding theological education in this moment of disruption in religion, in religion's social location in the culture, in higher education, and in the particular expression of both religion and higher education comprising theological education. The writers of the words of these chapters have worked exceptionally hard and exceedingly well over many decades to guide institutions, advocate on their behalf, raise money their missions required, participate in conversations about truth and goodness and grace, lead academic effort, and teach others about the work of theological schools. Theological schools are not educational bureaucracies, although their work is educational and their institutional structure requires bureaucratic disciplines. In the end, they are the work that people do with other people on behalf of still other people in service to God and God's hope for the human family.

This afterword is written at the conclusion of more than four decades of involvement in theological education. The authors of these chapters have been friends, colleagues, teachers, and companions with me through the years I served the Association of Theological Schools (ATS), most of them partners in shared efforts for all those years. Just as their words in these chapters provide thoughtful analyses of the current realities and possible future of theological education, their work in theological education across past decades provides helpful indicators about the characteristics of leadership that theological schools will require in the future. They are part of a cloud of witnesses, named and unnamed, many living and some of blessed memory, whose work and commitment I have observed over the years. On behalf of the thousands of people whose efforts have made the schools' work possible, this afterword celebrates the wisdom that their work and way of life has taught.

Barbara Wheeler has been as thoughtful a commentator on theological education as North American theological schools have had across these decades. Sensitive to the tendencies of theological school leaders to give too much attention to incidents and anecdotes and too little to facts and data, she founded and guided the only center dedicated to research on theological education—the Auburn Center for the Study of Theological Education. Under her guidance and typically by her own research, the center studied boards, faculty, administrators, students, and graduates. It examined the nature of leadership in these schools, their financial viability, characteristics associated with effective institutional advancement, and the public presence of these schools in the denominations and communities they serve. The center's work gave theological school leaders data that informed their leadership of institutions through decades of changes, pressures, and sometimes growth and expansion. She has been truthful and factual in her work and deeply faithful in her efforts. A person of unusually high standards, her work has consistently met and exceeded them. She has taught that the vision and values of theological schools that inspire their work require an informed grounding and understanding of the realities in which the vision and values can take flight.

Martha Horne not only understands Anglican life and witness but also is an Episcopal priest who embodies the best of that tradition. Like several other of these authors, she served a term as president of the ATS and in the role, chaired its board and worked closely with me. Institutions need wisdom to guide their work, address their problems, and contribute to the attainment of their missions. Martha provided all those in her work with the ATS. In her retirement from the Virginia Seminary, she served as dean of the ATS Presidents' Intensive and then guided a major project on theological school governance in changing times. Like most theological schools leaders, she had to oversee difficult decisions and moments, and when those moments came, her clarity, commitment, and integrity led the way and no doubt saved the day. She has been friend and mentor to many and an apt teacher, essential qualities in the leadership of theological institutions.

David Tiede is a student of the New Testament and served as a professor before being elected to the presidency of Luther Seminary. While he had studied the New Testament in great depth, he had never studied institutional leadership until it became his responsibility, a pattern that is characteristic of most leaders of theological schools. Once responsible, however, he studied the work of institutions as intensely as he had studied the New Testament. In one of the many moments of change faced by theological schools, he led Luther to think about its work in new ways to address needs that simply had not existed previously. Along the way, he thought a great deal about how institutions do their work and the role of governance as part of that work. He became a teacher of leadership and governance to other presidents and to the boards of many schools. The problems he solved during his long tenure as a seminary president are not the problems the school he led is facing now, but the principles of governance and leadership that he has taught are as valuable now as they were during his decades of leadership.

Donald Senior is also a New Testament scholar. He has written and lectured extensively on the New Testament and served on the Pontifical Biblical Commission, an entity that advises the pope and Holy See on Biblical teaching. He was not eager to serve as president of Catholic Theological Union but accepted the assignment from the religious communities who govern the school. He served with skill and dedication, as the best leaders of schools always do, and came to the conclusion of his term having accomplished a great deal for the school and ready to return to full-time teaching and writing. When the next chapter of the school proved destabilizing, he was asked once again to assume the presidency, which he did. He led during this second term with the same quiet competence that characterized the first, stabilized the school, and advanced it by raising the funds to build a much-needed facility for offices, a library, and classrooms. Like the best of presidents, he left the school much improved from where it was when he began, and for Don, that was doubly true. Ever the scholar, Don turned his attention to the ministry of administration in *The Gift of Administration*, which speaks wisely from biblical understanding about administration in service to mission.

Richard Mouw is perhaps the leading public intellectual of evangelical Protestantism. He speaks from the depth of philosophy, his academic area of expertise, to the breadth of his exceptionally accessible writing for Christians who have never read a book of academic philosophy or theology. The disruptions of this time have resulted in an American religion that seems muscular in its ability to curse but muted in its capacity to care. Rich has spoken to this tendency with a compelling call to civility. He and Barbara Wheeler are part of the same religious tradition but hold opposing views on an issue that was dividing their denomination. The two of them spoke at a number of conferences in which they explained their positions, discussed their differences, and shared their genuine affection for one another as brother and sister in faith. One can hope that theological education cultivates civility commensurate with conviction and humility proportionate to commitment. Serious study in service to the Gospel is not a new idea that Rich issued in his essay; it is both a pattern of his work and a call he has been issuing for decades.

Judith Berling was the chair of the ATS Commission on Accrediting when I began staffing the ATS work of accreditation in 1990. She was an academic officer in a complex institution with many moving parts and demonstrated considerable skill in attending to administrative issues and pursuing her scholarship in world religions. She taught me how to think about Christian ministry alongside other religions and how to begin to understand Asian religions and their cultural context. The ability to think Christianly, as Judith does, about the way other religions construct the holy, the sacred, the right, and the true is increasingly crucial for American theological education. For her, the hospitality of deep understanding of other religious visions is a way of being Christian, and like Richard Mouw's focus on civility, it is an increasing imperative in a world torn by religious differences. Judith has taught scores of PhD students over the years, and they carry the legacy of her scholarship to classrooms around the world.

I met Doug McConnell for the first time at a conference whose participants had come from around the world to discuss world Christianity as experienced and expressed by evangelical Protestants. He was a speaker who presented with considerable wisdom.

As an evangelical missionary and educator, the discussion of other world religions occurs in a different register for him than it does for mainline Protestants or Roman Catholics. Sharing the Gospel is a matter of heart and head, as Doug describes in his chapter, and sharing the Gospel faithfully requires tender treatment of the visions of the holy held by others. Doug is knowledgeable about and engaged in world Christianity, which is increasingly influenced by rapid growth in the majority world. Knowledge of the ethos and patterns of faith outside the West are increasingly crucial for any understanding of contemporary Christianity. As a global Christian, Doug is conversant with both the ways that Western Christians address other religions and the ways that majority world Christians address other religions, sometimes in the contexts of violence that are less evident in the West.

I hesitated to write about people who have written chapters of a book that is being published in honor of my work in theological education because it easily can be interpreted as an exercise in mutual admiration or tit-for-tat transaction. I have taken the risk of these paragraphs, however, both because I want to express my gratitude to these people who have been fellow travelers on a journey with me and because I think qualities evident in their work in the past are crucial for the work of theological education in the future.

First, they consistently have brought critical and engaging intellectual effort to this work. They have excelled in their respective academic fields and brought comparable acumen to their leadership of theological schools. The way forward will be paved with similar passion borne of good thinking and sensitive awareness. American religion, reflecting parts of American culture, has been flirting with the idea that intellectual effort is not needed as much as some technical know-how. Both are important, but from the parables of Jesus to the letters of Paul, from the books of Augustine and Aquinas to the commentaries of Luther, from the theology of Calvin to the sermons of Wesley, the Christian tradition has been deeply formed and well served by intellectual effort. The disruptions of the present moment will not be fully understood without careful analysis, and the future will only be hopeful if it is served by faithful, humble, and disciplined intellectual effort.

Second, these people have understood the value of institutions. The Christian project at its best is always a movement, a way in the world, a gathering of values and commitments, but its continuity across time is supported by institutions. The people who wrote these chapters have given huge effort to making institutions servants of a tradition. They have undertaken the many tasks this effort requires so that an institution could be faithful to the religious vocation to which it is called and for which it exists. Strange as it may seem, the more an institution is an agent of its calling, the less effort it gives to building itself up. It becomes strong to enhance its capacity to serve something beyond itself. These people, in different ways, from mainline Protestant, evangelical Protestant, and Roman Catholic visions of Christianity, built institutions that served the future of a tradition. Theological schools that serve a calling can change and greet the future with hope.

Third, they have demonstrated a commitment to faith and mission beyond career and status. Not all leaders are committed in this way, and across the years, the difference is noticeable. Leadership of a theological school brings a certain status with the constituency of the school and involves the exercise of the power institutions grant their leaders. The status and the power can be distracting, if not outright tempting, and the best leaders of theological schools avoid both the distraction and the temptation. They embody a singleness of purpose that reaches beyond personal ambition and institutional success and use institutional status and power to attain the institution's mission. Some leaders have a tendency to call attention to themselves; the best of them, however, direct attention to the vocation of the school they lead. The effect of this difference is especially palpable in a theological school.

These friends and authors are not the only people who have contributed to the attainment of the missions of theological schools. Countless students have sensed a leading to service or call to ministry that has required them to leave one place in life to pursue theological study for the next place in life. I continue to find great joy in talking with students. They are central to theological schools, and the Christian tradition needs their hope and passion, their knowledge and willingness to extend this tradition of faith for one more career, one more generation. I recently talked with a woman about to graduate with her MDiv. She had pursued a calling that had emerged early in her life, had been well educated, knew much, but perhaps more important, knew about what she did not know and was committed to learning as ministry began for her. She was eager to begin her service as an associate pastor soon after graduation.

Often, the most powerful experience students have in theological education is with the faculty. I find as much joy in professors I have known across the years as students. They have worked decades to gain the knowledge and wisdom necessary to guide a group of students sitting at tables in a seminar room or at desks in a classroom or in front of their computers in a virtual class. Most know the technical details of their disciplines, and the best of them understand that they educate students struggling with their own faith, calling, and sometimes trauma of life. They often engage students in their struggles, which is part of the reason that they are so influential. I reviewed a book by a young professor earlier this year. I had talked with this person about the possibility of pursuing PhD studies years ago, and this first book was a redevelopment of a dissertation study. It was scholarly but written nontechnically so it could be discussed by church groups. There are many kinds of scholarship necessary for theological study: some of it is technical and advances thought among scholars; some of it is accessible to people seeking to understand the faith they profess. The best professors are capable of both.

Administrators provide the institution's care for students, advance the institution's financial capacity, manage its financial resources carefully, maintain academic records, and support academic processes. Librarians attend to collections, acquire new titles, and lead in digital developments. Like faculty and students, I have known persons in all these roles, and what is true of the best of faculty is true of the best of them: they know their work and are doing what they do because they care about the mission of the school. I have met financial officers who left higher-paying jobs because they wanted to work in service to their faith, development officers who have turned down more lucrative positions with other institutions to remain at a theological school and give their energy to its mission.

Faculty, administrators, and theological school leaders know that work in religious institutions, like service in ministry, can be hazardous to their faith. Although they experience multiple sources of discouragement, they find ways to nurture their faith and mature the commitments that motivated them to take their various positions in theological education. There is no formula for remaining faithful, just the necessity of doing so. Across many years, I have been as impressed with the gifts of the Spirit that nurture and sustain persons in their work as I have been with the quality of their contributions and the tenacity of efforts.

In her introduction, Barbara Wheeler gives appropriate attention to the ways in which the content of these chapters can guide schools as they construct curricula that will transcend the disruptions of the current moment and lead schools toward a hopeful future. Faculty will need to think in new ways and reconstruct patterns of knowing. Curricula will need to veer from historical patterns. Future patterns of theological education will require individuals to work hard and use all their intellectual resources to envision educational designs that equip religious leaders to advance an ancient Gospel in a new cultural moment. It will be the work of many people, with their vast individual differences, and they become a curriculum as influential as courses and requirements.

Theological schools are places of ideas, new and old, sacred and profane. Ideas find their home in words—waves in the air, images in text. And in the Christian faith, the best words of faith find their homes in people of faith. And people of faith find their home in the purposes of God—partly made known in the past, partly realized in the present, and fully revealed only in a time yet to come.

CONTRIBUTORS

Daniel O. Aleshire retired as executive director of the Association of Theological Schools in 2017 after twenty-seven years of service with the association. Prior to his work with the Association of Theological Schools, he was a professor at the Southern Baptist Theological Seminary.

Judith A. Berling is professor emerita of Chinese and Comparative Religions at Graduate Theological Union, Berkeley.

Martha J. Horne is dean and president emerita of the Virginia Theological Seminary (Episcopal) in Alexandria, Virginia.

Douglas McConnell is Provost Emeritus, Professor of Leadership and Intercultural Studies, School of Intercultural Studies, Fuller Theological Seminary.

Richard J. Mouw is professor of Faith and Public Life at Fuller Theological Seminary, where he served as president from 1993 to 2013.

Rev. Donald Senior, CP, is president emeritus of Catholic Theological Union in Chicago, where he also serves as professor of New Testament and chancellor.

David L. Tiede is a professor of New Testament and president emeritus of Luther Seminary.

Barbara G. Wheeler, former president of Auburn Theological Seminary and founder of its Center for the Study of Theological Education, is a researcher and author of studies of theological education and church life.

NOTES

1: PROMISES TO SERVE

1 Martin Luther, "Ninety-Five Theses," in *Martin Luther's Basic Theological Writings*, ed. Timothy F. Lull (Minneapolis: Fortress, 1989), 21.

2 I have listed only schools accredited by the Association of Theological Schools (ATS), but there are other Lutheran denominations that do not require their ministers to attend ATS-accredited institutions. The Wisconsin Evangelical Lutheran Synod, as an example among others, has only recently acquired Associate Membership in the ATS. Their website identifies WELS as "a group of nearly 400,000 men, women, and children in nearly 1,300 congregations united by a common faith in Christ's saving love," hosting "ministerial education to provide workers for the more than 1,200 churches and 750 schools" primarily in the United States and Canada "through a system of four schools; two high-school-level preparatory schools, a college and a seminary."

3 Alasdair MacIntyre, *After Virtue*, 2nd ed. (Notre Dame: University of Notre Dame Press, 1981), 222.

4 See Hugh Heclo, *On Thinking Institutionally* (Boulder: Paradigm, 2008), 107: "Institutions are an inheritance of valued purpose and moral obligation, they constitute socially ordered groundings for human life."

5 The Lutherans who immigrated to South Carolina, for example, never forgot the "salt oaths" they took as they fled Austria to protect their children from coerced conversions to Roman Catholicism. And the Missouri Synod's confessional identity sustained their refusal of the Prussian mandate

for union with the Reformed tradition. Some Norwegian and German immigrants to the Midwest also remembered opposition to the Lutheran state churches, perpetuating Hans Nielsen Hauge's free church and the evangelical missionary zeal of Wilhelm Loehe.

6 "Ecclesia Plantanda" was the motto of Henry Melchior Muhlenberg (1711–87), who is often called the patriarch of North American Lutherans.

7 See Eric W. Gritsch and Robert W. Jenson, *Lutheranism* (Philadelphia: Fortress, 1976), 119: "The ordained minister of the gospel is one called by the congregation . . . to 'minister' to the gospel itself, as the word upon which the community depends . . . to *tend* the life of the gospel in the congregation, to care for its vivacity and authenticity."

8 Collaborations in the 1960s between church leaders and seminary faculties helped bring the former American Lutheran Church through conflicts about historical research and biblical authority, but these concerns divided the Lutheran Church Missouri Synod, yielding a seminary in exile (Seminex) and a new synod (the American Evangelical Lutheran Church), which later merged into the Evangelical Lutheran Church in America (ELCA). Lutheran theological teachers in all traditions have regularly been called upon to help their churches to deal with complex ecumenical proposals and policies regarding human sexuality.

9 In addition to resources in catechetical and adult education, which often reached beyond the Lutheran churches, Lutheran Scripture scholars have contributed widely in academic and church circles. Popular studies (e.g., Bethel Bible Series, Word and Witness, Crossways, Search, and Book of Faith) have had ecumenical and global usage.

10 See Lesslie Newbigin, *Proper Confidence* (Grand Rapids: Eerdmans, 1995), 28.

11 See James Samuel Preus, *From Shadow to Promise* (Cambridge, MA: Belknap, 1969).

12 It is not an accident that the promise of Alcoholics Anonymous is similarly anchored in facing the undeniable truth of addiction on the pathway to recovery.

13 The "theology of the cross" is a testimony to God's ultimate self-disclosure in the death of the Messiah Jesus, moving us in Christ deeper than our even troubled introspective consciences will tolerate and to the hope in God that lies beyond our human agency.

14 See Douglas John Hall, *Thinking the Faith: Christian Theology in a North American Context* (Minneapolis: Augsburg, 1989), 164: "The power of doctrinaire optimism should not be underestimated. . . . This same insistent and official optimism about the future . . . on account of whose grave

insecurity and striving for the control of that future the world is dangerously imperiled."

15 Echoing Luther and the Apostle Paul, Lutheran speech is full of references to God's Law and Gospel. This rhetoric has at times abetted misunderstandings of the place of the Old and New Testaments in Christian theology. This ignorance has led some Lutherans to neglect Israel's Scriptures, forgetting that Martin Luther's insight in reading Paul was deeply informed by his scholarship in Genesis, Isaiah, and Psalms. Law and Gospel are testimonies to how the authority (power) of God's word addresses us as command and promise, revealing the reality of our human situation in the presence of God and our neighbor and calling us to faith in Christ Jesus.

16 See Scott Hendrix, *Recultivating the Vineyard: The Reformation Agendas of Christendom* (Louisville: John Knox, 2004).

17 Robert W. Bertram, "How a Lutheran Does Theology: Some Clues from the Lutheran Confessions," in *Lutheran-Episcopal Dialogue: Report and Recommendations*, ed. William G. Weinhauer and Robert L. Wietelman (Cincinnati: Forward Movement, 1981), 87. See also Jukka A. Kääriäinen, *Mission Shaped by Promise: Lutheran Missiology Confronts the Challenge of Religious Pluralism* (Wipf and Stock, 2012); Kääriäinen, "Mission," in *Gift and Promise: The Augsburg Confession and the Heart of Christian Theology*, ed. Edward H. Schroeder, Ronald Neustadt, and Stephen Hitchcock (Minneapolis: Fortress, 2016), 175–95.

18 Mark D. Tranvik, trans., *The Freedom of a Christian* (Minneapolis: Augsburg, 2008), 50.

19 When the Gestapo shut down the Finkenwalde seminary in 1938, Dietrich Bonhoeffer wrote *Life Together* (Dietrich Bonhoeffer Works, vol. 5, ed. Geffrey B. Kelly, trans. Daniel W. Bloesch and James H. Burtness [Minneapolis: Fortress, 1996]), providing a glimpse of the formation of pastoral leadership in visible community with other Christians. His testimony in that hostile setting alerts theological schools in often indifferent contexts: "The Christian cannot simply take for granted the privilege of living among other Christians" (27).

20 Loren Mead, *The Once and Future Church* (Washington, DC: Alban Institute, 1991).

21 Martin Luther loved music and wrote many hymns. Johann Sebastian Bach, often called the fifth evangelist, set high musical and theological standards for this heritage of choirs, organs, and congregational singing. The North American Lutheran college choirs continue to receive public recognition, and with his whimsical teasing of their "blandness," public radio's Garrison Keillor marked out how "Lutherans are bred from childhood to sing

in four-part harmony. It's a talent that comes from sitting on the lap of someone singing alto or tenor or bass and hearing the harmonic intervals by putting your little head against that person's rib cage"; "Singing with the Lutherans" is available on multiple websites.

22 Lutheran Services in America (LSA) is a national network of Lutheran service providers that annually provide approximate $21 billion in care, serving six million people. The LSA agencies collaborate constantly with Catholic Charities and a host of other human care organizations. With offices in Washington, DC, LSA hosts public policy discussions and advocates for human need with Congress and the nation's administration. Since 1939, Lutheran Immigration and Refugee Services (LIRS) has helped resettle more than five hundred thousand "displaced persons" from Europe after World War II; Korean orphans; Vietnamese boat people; and Laotian, Ethiopian, and Syrian refugees in recent decades. This mission of human care has endured with local resettlement support, never without criticism. And Lutheran World Relief (LWR) identifies itself as "empowered by God's unconditional love in Jesus Christ" to help US Lutherans serve their neighbors overseas who face poverty, injustice, and human suffering, reaching 3,467,823 people in thirty-two countries in 2016.

23 A Lutheran seminary professor, Foster R. McCurley, was the first to design and fill this role. See Foster R. McCurley, ed., *Social Ministry in the Lutheran Tradition* (Minneapolis: Fortress, 2008).

24 Download the online version of the LSS-MN publication "My Neighbor Is Muslim." Written by faculty from Luther College and Luther Seminary, this resource is being used widely as a primer for "Exploring the Muslim Faith," http://www.lirs.org/myneighborismuslim/.

25 See Clayton M. Christensen and Henry J. Eyring, *The Innovative University: Changing the DNA of Higher Education from the Inside Out* (San Francisco: Jossey-Bass, 2011); Jeffrey J. Selingo, *College (Un)bound: The Future of Higher Education and What It Means for Students* (Boston: New Harvest, 2013).

26 See the essays by Paul Dovre and Mark Schwehn in *The Future of Religious Colleges*, ed. Paul Dovre (Grand Rapids: Eerdmans, 2002).

27 Tom Christenson, *The Gift and Task of Lutheran Higher Education* (Minneapolis: Augsburg Fortress, 2004), 197n9.

28 Darrell Jodock, "The Third Path, Religious Diversity, and Civil Discourse," in *The Vocation of Lutheran Higher Education*, ed. Jason Mahn (Edina, MN: Lutheran University Press, 2016), 82–98.

29 The Strommen Center for Meaningful Work at Augsburg University is an excellent example.

30 Daniel O. Aleshire, *Earthen Vessels: Hopeful Reflections on the World and Future of Theological Schools* (Grand Rapids: Eerdmans, 2008), 160.

31 Thomas L. Friedman, *Thank You for Being Late* (New York: Farrar, Straus, and Giroux, 2016), 19–35.

32 ATS Commission on Accrediting, General Institutional Standards, Standard 3.1.1, "Goals of the Theological Curriculum."

33 In 2017, Luther Seminary, the largest of the ELCA seminaries, now producing 40 percent of its clergy, completed a substantial curriculum reform. Luther is also welcoming the campus presence of Augsburg University's graduate programs, "yoked" with Augsburg in shared systems of administrative support. In 2012, the Lutheran School of Theology in Chicago welcomed three graduate programs and an immigration law clinic to its campus from Valparaiso University in Indiana. LSTC is also seeking to address its need for sustainability and campus improvement, currently entering the public phase of a capital campaign.

In 2017, Wartburg Theological Seminary began its Master of Divinity Collaborative Learning Program with "a new pathway of learning for students with a strong partnership between the seminary, synods, and congregations." As these three ELCA seminaries are regrouping deeply from within and in relationship with their constituencies, the other four ELCA schools are being systemically reconfigured in their governance, ownership, and leadership, as well as in their educational profiles.

In 2012, Lutheran Theological Southern Seminary in Columbia, South Carolina, merged with Lenoir Rhyne University in Hickory, North Carolina. It has already experienced leadership changes. In 2014 Pacific Lutheran Theological Seminary in the Graduate Theological Union in Berkeley became a graduate school of California Lutheran University. They are relocating their campus in Berkeley, and their second new executive began as rector on June 1, 2017. The Lutheran Theological Seminary in Philadelphia and Gettysburg Lutheran Theological Seminary concluded their merger as United Lutheran Seminary with their new president beginning July 1, 2017, still operating on two campuses. And earlier in 2107, Trinity Lutheran Seminary and Capital University in Columbus, Ohio, completed their mergers as a "reunion," welcoming a new dean for the seminary.

34 See Andrew Pettegree, *Brand Luther* (Penguin Books, 2016).

35 See such classic studies in Christian mission and culture as Lamin Sanneh, *Translating the Message: The Missionary Impact on Culture* (Maryknoll, NY: Orbis Books, 1989); David J. Bosch, *Transforming Mission* (Maryknoll, NY: Orbis Books, 1991).

36 Friedman's reflections ("The Frozen Chosen") on his Jewish upbringing in St. Louis Park, Minnesota, move far beyond sentiment to a testimony to the human hope of trustworthy communities.

37 Along with the educational resources of the Association of Theological Schools and the Auburn Center, the schools have continued to learn from the excellent materials of the Association of Governing Boards (AGB); the *In Trust* magazine and consulting from In Trust Center for Theological Studies; and Richard P. Chait, William P. Ryan, and Barbara E. Taylor, *Governance as Leadership: Reframing the Work of Nonprofit Boards* (New Jersey: Board Source, 2005).

38 Luther, "Ninety-Five Theses," 21.

39 An early title of this essay was "Promises to Keep," with allusions to Robert Frost's poem "Stopping by the Woods on a Snowy Evening": "The woods are lovely, dark and deep, but I have promises to keep, and miles to go before I sleep." Beautiful as that script of human agency may be, the master narrative of the Christian faith is trust in God, who made and keeps the promises. The faithful work of Lutheran theological education is defined by "What serves Christ."

2: FROM CANTERBURY TO CAPETOWN

1 Several additional Episcopal seminaries were established in the nineteenth century and two in the twentieth century. As of this writing, there are ten accredited Episcopal seminaries in the US, with several resulting from the merger of earlier schools.

2 Michael Hout and Tom W. Smith, "Fewer Americans Affiliate with Organized Religions, Belief and Practice Unchanged: Key Findings from the 2014 General Social Survey" (Press Summary, March 10, 2015), 1.

3 Hout and Smith, 1–2.

4 Tobin Grant is a political science professor at Southern Illinois University and associate editor of the *Journal for the Scientific Study of Religion*. For this blog post, see Religion News Service, http://religionnews.com/2015/03/12/analysis-7-5-million-americans-lost-religion-since-2012.

5 Hout and Smith, "General Social Survey," 2.

6 Emma Green, "How Will Young People Choose Their Religion?," *Atlantic*, March 20, 2016, https://www.theatlantic.com/politics/archive/2016/03/how-will-young-people-choose-their-religion/474366/.

7 Green, 1.

8 Becka A. Alper, "Millennials Are Less Religious Than Older Americans, but Just as Spiritual," November 23, 2015, http://www.pewresearch.org/fact-tank/2015/11/23/millennials-are-less-religious-than-older-americans-but-just-as-spiritual/.

9 "Episcopal Domestic Fast Fact Trends, 2011–2015," http://www
   .episcopalchurch.org/page/research-and-statistics.

10 "The Anglican Way: Signposts on a Common Journey," May 2007, http://
   www.anglicancommunion.org/media/109378/The-Anglican-Way-Sign
   posts-on-a-Common-Journey_en.pdf.

11 "The Anglican Way," 2.

12 Discussions of an "Anglican Way" often begin by naming Scripture, tradition, and reason as the three authoritative sources for Anglican doctrine and
   teaching, but Scripture has always held the primary position as the unique
   self-revelation of God.

13 Article VI, "Of the Sufficiency of the Holy Scriptures for Salvation," of the
   Thirty-Nine Articles of Religion, as printed in *Articles of Religion in the Book of
   Common Prayer, According to the Use of the Episcopal Church* (New York: Oxford
   University Press, 1979), 868.

14 *The Chicago Lambeth Quadrilateral 1886, 1888*, as found in the *Book of Common
   Prayer*, 876–77. In addition to Scripture, three other essentials are named:
   "The Nicene Creed as the sufficient statement of the Christian Faith, the
   two Sacraments—Baptism and the Supper of the Lord ministered with
   unfailing use of Christ's words of institution and of the elements ordained
   by Him, and he Historic Episcopate, locally adapted in the methods of its
   administration to the varying needs of the nations and peoples called of God
   into the unity of His Church."

15 Liturgies for the ordination of deacons, priests, and bishops in *Book of Common Prayer*, 510–55.

16 *Book of Common Prayer*, 236, Proper 28.

17 In his book *Anglican Approaches to Scripture from the Reformation to the Present*
   (New York: Crossroads, 2006), Rowan Greer describes various ways in
   which Anglicans have interpreted Scripture and why it is difficult to speak
   of a single view of Scripture or a single Anglican perspective.

18 Greer, 162.

19 From 1968 Lambeth Conference Reports in Stephen W. Sykes, *The Integrity
   of Anglicanism* (London: Mowbray, 1978), 9.

20 *Bonds of affection* is the term traditionally used to describe the relationships
   among the provinces of the Anglican Communion, signifying the familial
   nature of the relationships among provinces that share a common heritage.

21 Clare Amos, ed., *The Bible in the Life of the Church* (London: Canterbury Press
   Norwich, 2013).

22 "Reading Scripture Together across the Anglican Communion: Why
   and How?," http://www.anglicancommunion.org/ministry/theological/
   bible/, 2.

23 Allister Sparks and Mpho Tutu, *Tutu Authorized* (Auckland, New Zealand: PQ Blackwell, 2011), 73–75.

24 *Lex orandi, lex credendi*, a central tenet of Anglicanism, expresses the understanding that our liturgy is an expression of our theology.

25 Samuel Wells, "How Common Worship Forms Local Character," *Studies in Christian Ethics* 15, no. 1 (2002): 67, journals.sagepub.com/doi/pdf/10 .1177/095394680201500106.

26 Charles Price and Louis Weil, *Liturgy for Living* (New York: Seabury, 1979), 54.

27 J. Eileen Scully, "Theological Education for the Anglican Communion: The Promises and Challenges of TEAC," *Anglican Theological Review* 90, no. 2 (Spring 2008): 217.

28 Episcopal Church's Office of Research, "Transforming Churches," https:// www.episcopalchurch.org/library/topics/transforming-churches.

29 C. Kirk Hadaway, *New Facts on Episcopal Church Growth and Decline* (New York: Domestic and Foreign Missionary Society, 2015), 8.

30 Hadaway, 12–13.

31 Sheryl Kujawa-Holbrook has written extensively about young adults. In her article "Worship, Music, and Generational Conflict" (in *Looking Forward: Theological Education, Young Adults, and the 21st-Century Church*, vol. 32, no. 2), she notes the desire of young adults to make a difference in the world and to see a connection between the church's liturgy and its response to the needs of the world (http://www.faithformationlearningexchange.net/ uploads/5/2/4/6/5246709/young_adults__21st_century_church.pdf).

32 An example is the Iona School in Texas, created in partnership with the Diocese of Texas and the Seminary of the Southwest, providing training for deacons and part-time or bivocational priests for dioceses in the southern, southwestern, and western states of the US.

33 Anglican Consultative Council, "Marks of Mission," http://www .anglicancommunion.org/mission/marks-of-mission.asp.

34 Ellen Davis is professor of Bible and Practical Theology at Duke University Divinity School. Since 2004 she has organized groups of students and faculty to travel to the Diocese of Renk in Southern Sudan to teach short courses in summers and between terms. Davis and Jo Bailey Wells led five multiday sessions studying biblical texts with Anglicans in different towns in Southern Sudan in 2010 and 2011 as part of the Bible in the Life of the Church project.

35 Greer, *Anglican Approaches*, 162.

3: THE ECCLESIAL VISION OF POPE FRANCIS AND THE FUTURE OF CATHOLIC THEOLOGICAL EDUCATION

1 This includes what is called the *Ratio Fundamentalis*, a policy document produced by Vatican Congregation of the Clergy, the office responsible for overseeing priestly formation in the worldwide Catholic community. An updated version of the *Ratio*, titled *The Gift of the Priestly Vocation*, was published in December 2016. It too is built on the four pillars of priestly formation outlined by Pope John Paul II. On the abiding influence of *Pastores Dabo Vobis*, see further K. Schuth, *Seminary Formation: Recent History, Current Circumstances, New Directions* (Collegeville: Liturgical, 2016), esp. 9–32.

2 *Pastores Dabo Vobis*, pars. 43–44.

3 *Pastores Dabo Vobis*, pars. 45–50.

4 *Pastores Dabo Vobis*, par. 45.

5 *Pastores Dabo Vobis*, pars. 51–56.

6 *Pastores Dabo Vobis*, par. 51.

7 *Pastores Dabo Vobis*, pars. 57–59.

8 "The four areas of formation—human, spiritual, intellectual, and pastoral—that provide a framework for the formation of deacons and priests provide a framework for lay ecclesial ministers as well"; *Co-workers in the Vineyard of the Lord: A Resource for Guiding the Development of Lay Ecclesial Ministry* (Washington, DC: United States Conference of Catholic Bishops, 2005), 33.

9 The Synod's focus was on what is called the "New Evangelization," which accentuates the need to reinvigorate those who are already Christian, even if in a nominal way. Pope Francis's focus in *The Joy of the Gospel*, however, is much more outward directed and describes evangelization as an outward missionary impulse.

10 *Joy of the Gospel*, par. 10. Here the pope is quoting a powerful statement of the Latin American bishops, referred to as the Aparecida document of 2007, a statement of the Latin American Bishops' Conference that the then cardinal Jorge Bergolio played a major part in formulating.

11 See the description of this incident in Austin Ivereigh, *The Great Reformer: Francis and the Making of a Radical Pope* (New York: Holt, Henry, 2014).

12 *Joy of the Gospel*, par. 120.

13 *Joy of the Gospel*, pars. 135–59.

14 See Gregory Heille, OP, *The Preaching of Pope Francis: Missionary Discipleship and the Ministry of the Word* (Collegeville: Liturgical, 2015).

15 *Joy of the Gospel*, par. 198.

16 "Be praised, my Lord, for all your creation" is a recurring phrase throughout the Canticle, said to be composed by Francis in 1224.

17 *Laudato Si'*, par. 92.

18 *Laudato Si'*, par. 217.

19 *Laudato Si'*, par. 215.

20 *Laudato Si'*, par. 231.

21 *Laudato Si'*, par. 231.

22 *Laudato Si'*, pars. 230–31.

23 *Amoris Laetitia*, par. 295.

24 *Amoris Laetitia*, par. 296. The phrases in quotation marks are from the Synod's own recommendations on which the pope comments.

25 *Amoris Laetitia*, par. 297.

26 *Amoris Laetitia*, par. 308.

27 *Amoris Laetitia*, par. 309.

28 *Amoris Laetitia*, par. 310.

29 *Amoris Laetitia*, par. 312.

30 K. Schuth, *Seminary Formation*, 118.

31 For an elaboration of what is meant by a "culture of encounter," see the essay of Msgr. Peter Vaccari, "The Culture of Encounter: The Future of Seminary Formation," in K. Schuth, *Seminary Formation*, 164–73.

32 *Joy of the Gospel*, par. 262.

33 A recent project fostered by Cardinal Gianfranco Ravasi, the head of the Pontifical Council for Culture, stresses the importance of appreciation for beauty in art, literature, and architecture in the training of priests and other church ministers. The church, he notes, has long held a belief in the important connection between art and faith, which are "like sisters, because they both have as their main task to try not only to represent what can be seen, or the surface of things, but also to find the more profound sense." Quoted in *Crux: Taking the Catholic Pulse*, January 30, 2017.

34 The pope has also noted that professional lay ministers themselves can be infected by what he calls the "leprosy" of clericalism—exhibiting the same kind of closed, elitist, and "overly professional" approach to mission.

35 *Joy of the Gospel*, par. 251 (the pope also quotes here his predecessor John Paul II).

36 "Jesus Christ is the face of the Father's mercy. These words might well sum up the mystery of the Christian faith." Pope Francis's statement of April 11, 2015, inaugurating the Year of Mercy.

37 *Amoris Laetitia*, par. 311.

4: BROADENING THE EVANGELICAL VISION

1 John Henry Newman, *The Idea of a University* (New York: Rinehart, 1960), 126.

2 Quoted in Richard Hofstadter, *Anti-intellectualism in American Life* (New York: Vintage Books, 1963), 103.

3 Quoted by William Ringenberg, *The Christian College: A History of Protestant Higher Education in America* (Grand Rapids: Eerdmans, 1984), 165.

4 Ernest B. Gordon, *Adoniram Judson Gordon: A Biography, with Letters and Illustrative Extracts Drawn from Unpublished or Uncollected Sermons and Addresses* (New York: Fleming H. Revell, 1896), 171–72.

5 Virginia Brereton, *Training God's Army: The American Bible School, 1880–1940* (Bloomington: University of Indiana Press, 1990), 62.

6 Mark A. Noll, "The Divine Doctor" [interview with Jaroslav Pelikan], *Christianity Today* 34, no. 12 (September 10, 1990): 26.

7 Stephen Ellingson, *The Megachurch and the Mainline: Remaking Religious Tradition in the Twenty-First Century* (Chicago: University of Chicago Press, 2007), 185.

8 Paul Goldberg, "The Gospel of Church Architecture, Revised," *New York Times*, April 20, 1995, http://www.nytimes.com/1995/04/20/garden/the-gospel-of-church-architecture-revised.html?pagewanted=all.

9 John Calvin, *Institutes of the Christian Religion* I.III.1, ed. John T. McNeill, trans. Ford Lewis Battles, Library of Christian Classics 20 (Philadelphia: Westminster, 1960), 44.

10 Augustine, *Confessions*, bk. 1, chap. 1, http://www.magister.msk.ru/library/bible/comment/augustin/augus01e.htm.

11 Calvin, *Institutes*, I.XI.8.

12 No one has been able to find that comment in Chesterton's writings, but it does show up in a piece by a lesser-known author: http://www.chesterton.org/qmeister2/qmeister.htm.

5: EVANGELICALS, MISSION, AND MULTIFAITH EDUCATION

1 Evelyne A. Reisacher, *Joyful Witness in the Muslim World: Sharing the Gospel in Everyday Encounters* (Grand Rapids: Baker Academic, 2016).

2 Farida Saidi, "A Study of Current Leadership Styles in the North African Church" (PhD diss., Fuller Theological Seminary, School of Intercultural Studies, 2010).

3 Stephen R. Graham, "Christian Hospitality and Pastoral Practices in a Multifaith Society: An ATS Project, 2010–2012," *Theological Education* 47, no. 1 (2012): 9. Volume 47, number 1 of *Theological Education* provides significant insights on the process and outcomes of ATS project on Christian hospitality.

4 ATS degree revised program standard A.2.3.2 for the master of divinity degree, June 2012.

5 Daniel O. Aleshire, *Earthen Vessels: Hopeful Reflections on the Work and Future of Theological Schools* (Grand Rapids: Eerdmans, 2008), 168.

6 Aleshire, 5.

7 For the broader challenge of multifaith education, see Judith A. Berling, "What about Other Religions? Opportunities and Challenges in Mainline Theological Education," in this volume.

8 See Mark Labberton, ed., *Still Evangelical? Insiders Reconsider Political, Social, and Theological Meaning* (Downers Grove, IL: IVP, 2018).

9 David W. Bebbington, *Evangelicalism in Modern Britain: A History from the 1730s to the 1980s* (London: Unwin Hyman, 1989), 2–3.

10 Graham, "Christian Hospitality and Pastoral Practices," 5.

11 Scott W. Sunquist, *Understanding Christian Mission: Participation in Suffering and Glory* (Grand Rapids: Baker Academic, 2013), 173.

12 Darrell Whiteman, "Anthropology and Mission: An Incarnational Connection," *International Journal of Frontier Missions* 21, no. 2 (Summer 2004): 79–88.

13 Terry Muck and Frances S. Adeney, *Christianity Encountering World Religions: The Practice of Mission in the Twenty-First Century* (Grand Rapids: Baker Academic, 2009).

14 Veli-Matti Kärkkäinen, *A Constructive Christian Theology for the Pluralistic World*, 5 vols. (Grand Rapids: Eerdmans).

15 Amos Yong, *Beyond the Impasse: Toward a Pneumatological Theology of Religions* (Eugene, OR: Wipf and Stock, 2014).

16 Richard J. Mouw, *Uncommon Decency: Christian Civility in an Uncivil World*, rev. and exp. ed. (Downers Grove, IL: IVP, 2010); Christine Pohl, *Making Room: Recovering Hospitality as a Christian Tradition* (Grand Rapids: Eerdmans, 1999). The pedagogical significance of these two volumes is discussed at length in Douglas McConnell, "Educating Seminarians for Convicted Civility in a Multifaith World," *Teaching Theology & Religion* 16, no. 4 (October 2013): 329–37; and Sang-Ehil Han, Paul Louis Metzger, and Terry C. Muck, "Christian Hospitality and Pastoral Practice from an Evangelical Perspective," *Theological Education* 47, no. 1 (2012): 11–32.

17 Student posting on Canvas, November 14, 2017, IS503 Practices of Mission.

18 See Judith A. Berling's excellent overview of the impact of multifaith education in this volume, "What about Other Religions? Opportunities and Challenges in Mainline Theological Education."

19 *Teaching Theology & Religion* 16, no. 4.

20 Justus Baird, "Multifaith Education in American Theological Schools: Looking Back, Looking Ahead," *Teaching Theology & Religion* 16, no. 4 (October 2013): 309–21.

21 Baird, 318.

22 Student posting on Canvas, November 17, 2017, IS503 Practices of Mission.

23 See Richard J. Mouw and Robert L. Millet, eds., *Talking Doctrine: Mormons and Evangelicals in Conversation* (Downers Grove, IL: InterVarsity, 2015), for reflections on our experience.

24 Baird, "Multifaith Education," 318.

25 Edward Mote, "My Hope Is Built," https://www.umcdiscipleship.org/resources/history-of-hymns-my-hope-is-built.

26 Baird, "Multifaith Education," 318.

27 Richard J. Mouw, *Uncommon Decency: Christian Civility in an Uncivil World*, rev. and exp. ed. (Downers Grove, IL: IVP, 2010).

28 McConnell, "Educating Seminarians," 330–31.

29 Student posting on Canvas, January 18, 2018, MR549 Evangelicals and Interfaith Dialogue.

30 Timothy C. Tennent, *Christianity at the Religious Roundtable: Evangelicalism in Conversation with Hinduism, Buddhism, and Islam* (Grand Rapids: Baker Academic, 2001), 249.

31 Allen Yeh, *Polycentric Missiology: Twenty-First Century Mission from Everyone to Everywhere* (Downers Grove, IL: IVP Academic, 2016).

32 Yeh, 215.

33 Baird, "Multifaith Education," 319.

6: WHAT ABOUT OTHER RELIGIONS?

1 Will Herberg, *Protestant, Catholic, Jew: An Essay in American Religious Sociology* (Garden City, NY: Doubleday, 1955).

2 Judith A. Berling, *Understanding Other Religious Worlds: A Guide for Interreligious Education* (Maryknoll, NY: Orbis Books, 2004), 5.

3 Diana Eck, *A New Religious America: How a "Christian Country" Has Become the World's Most Religiously Diverse Nation* (New York: HarperCollins, 2001).

4 *Teaching Theology & Religion* 16, no. 3 (October 2013).

5 Justus Baird, "Multifaith Education in American Theological Schools: Looking Back, Looking Forward," *Teaching Theology & Religion* 16, no. 3 (October 2013): 309–21.

6 Baird, 310.

7 Baird, 310.

8 Eboo Patel, *Interfaith Leadership: A Primer* (Boston: Beacon Press, 2016), 5.

9 Patel.

10 Stephen Graham, *Reflections for the Meeting of "The Current State of Interfaith Education in the United States"* (New York: Henry Luce Foundation, September 21, 2015), 2.

11 Graham, 3.

12 Baird, "Multifaith Education," 320.

13 Elinor Pierce, "Beyond Common Ground: The Pluralism Project at Harvard University," paper presented at meeting on the Current State of Interreligious Education in the United States, at the Henry Luce Foundation, September 21, 2015.

14 Jennifer Howe Peace, "Religious Self, Religious Other: Coformation as a Model for Interreligious Education," paper presented at meeting on Critical Issues in Interreligious Education in the United States, Graduate Theological Union, March 21–23, 2017.

15 Munir Jiwa, "Islamic Studies in the Interreligious Context of the Graduate Theological Union," paper presented at meeting on Critical Issues in Interreligious Education in the United States, March 21–23, Graduate Theological Union, Berkeley, California, 8–9.

16 Mary C. Boys and Sara S. Lee, "The Catholic-Jewish Colloquium: An Experiment in Interreligious Learning," *Religious Education* 91, no. 4 (Fall 1996): 421–66.

17 Rachel Mikva, "Reflections in the Waves: How Feminist/Womanist/Mujerista Theory Informs the Pedagogy of Interreligious Studies," presented at meeting on Critical Issues in Interreligious Education in the United States, Graduate Theological Union, Berkeley, California, March 21–23, 2017.

18 See, for example, Pim Valkenburg, "Learning with and from Religious Others," *Teaching Theology & Religion* 16, no. 4 (October 2013): 391.

19 I have included a variety of pedagogical strategies, and some discussions about their limitations, in chapter 6 ("Classroom Learning") of *Understanding Other Religious Worlds*, 81–109.

20 Berling, *Understanding Other Religious Worlds*, 73–80.

21 Private conversation with colleague teaching at a major evangelical school.

22 Nancy Fuchs Kreimer, "Interreligious Education at Reconstructionist Rabbinical College: Thirty Years of Experiments, Exploration, and Evolution," presented at meeting on Critical Issues in Interreligious Education in the United States, Graduate Theological Union, Berkeley, California, March 21–23, 2017.

23 Mary Hess, "The Pastoral Practice of Christian Hospitality as Presence in Muslim-Christian Engagement: Contextualizing the Classroom," *Theological Education* 47, no. 2 (2013): 7–12.

24 Personal communication with Mary Hess, June 2016.

25 See, for example, Robert Wuthnow, *The Restructuring of American Religion* (Princeton: Princeton University Press, 1988).

26 Cynthia Bourgeault, *The Wisdom Jesus: Transforming Heart and Mind—a New Perspective on Christ and His Message* (Boston: Shambhala, 2008), 25.

27 William Christian, *Local Religion in Sixteenth-Century Spain* (Princeton: Princeton University Press, 1981).

28 Robert A. Orsi, *Between Heaven and Earth: The Religious Worlds People Make and the Scholars Who Study Them* (Princeton: Princeton University Press, 2005).

29 See Richard Madsen, *China and Christianity: Burdened Past, Hopeful Future* (Armonk, NY: M. E. Sharpe, 2001).

30 Roger Lipsey, "What Is the Spiritual in Art?" and "Abstraction—a Religious Art, Sometimes," in *An Art of Our Own: The Spiritual in Twentieth Century Art* (Boston: Shambhala, 1988), 1–28; and Charlene Spretnak, "1945 to the Present—Allusive Spirituality," in *Spiritual Dynamic in Modern Art: Art History Reconsidered, 1800 to the Present* (New York: Palgrave Macmillan, 2014), 125–49.

31 Wilfred Cantwell Smith, *Towards a World Theology: Faith and the Comparative History of Religion* (Philadelphia: Westminster, 1981; Maryknoll, NY: Orbis Books, 1989), v, 24–25.

BIBLIOGRAPHY

Aleshire, Daniel O. *Earthen Vessels: Hopeful Reflection on the World and Future of Theological Schools.* Grand Rapids: Eerdmans, 2008.

Alper, Becka A. "Millennials Are Less Religious Than Older Americans, but Just as Spiritual." Pew Research Center. November 23, 2015. http://www.pewresearch.org/fact-tank/2015/11/23/millennials-are-less-religious-than-older-americans-but-just-as-spiritual/.

Amos, Clare, ed. *The Bible in the Life of the Church.* London: Canterbury Press Norwich, 2013.

Articles of Religion in the Book of Common Prayer, According to the Use of the Episcopal Church. New York: Oxford University Press, 1979.

Augustine. *Confessions.* http://www.magister.msk.ru/library/bible/comment/augustin/augus01e.htm.

Baird, Justus. "Multifaith Education in American Theological Schools: Looking Back, Looking Ahead." *Teaching Theology & Religion* 16, no. 4 (October 2013): 309–21.

———. "Multifaith Education in American Theological Schools: Looking Back, Looking Forward." *Teaching Theology & Religion* 16, no. 3 (October 2013): 309–21.

Bebbington, David W. *Evangelicalism in Modern Britain: A History from the 1730s to the 1980s.* London: Unwin Hyman, 1989.

Berling, Judith A. *Understanding Other Religious Worlds: A Guide for Interreligious Education.* Maryknoll, NY: Orbis Books, 2004.

Bertram, Robert W. "How a Lutheran Does Theology: Some Clues from the Lutheran Confessions." In *Lutheran-Episcopal Dialogue: Report and Recommendations*, edited by William G. Weinhauer and Robert L. Wietelman. Cincinnati: Forward Movement, 1981.

Bonhoeffer, Dietrich. *Dietrich Bonhoeffer Works*. Vol. 5, *Life Together*, edited by Geffrey B. Kelly, translated by Daniel W. Bloesch and James H. Burtness. Minneapolis: Fortress, 1996.

Bosch, David J. *Transforming Mission*. Maryknoll, NY: Orbis Books, 1991.

Bourgeault, Cynthia. *The Wisdom Jesus: Transforming Heart and Mind—a New Perspective on Christ and His Message*. Boston: Shambhala, 2008.

Boys, Mary C., and Sara S. Lee. "The Catholic-Jewish Colloquium: An Experiment in Interreligious Learning." *Religious Education* 91, no. 4 (Fall 1996): 421–66.

Brereton, Virginia. *Training God's Army: The American Bible School, 1880–1940*. Bloomington: University of Indiana Press, 1990.

Calvin, John. *Institutes of the Christian Religion*. Edited by John T. McNeill, translated by Ford Lewis Battles. Philadelphia: Westminster, 1960.

Chait, Richard P., William P. Ryan, and Barbara E. Taylor. *Governance as Leadership: Reframing the Work of Nonprofit Boards*. New Jersey: Board Source, 2005.

Christensen, Clayton M., and Henry J. Eyring. *The Innovative University: Changing the DNA of Higher Education from the Inside Out*. San Francisco: Jossey-Bass, 2011.

Christenson, Tom. *The Gift and Task of Lutheran Higher Education*. Minneapolis: Augsburg Fortress, 2004.

Christian, William. *Local Religion in Sixteenth-Century Spain*. Princeton: Princeton University Press, 1981.

Co-workers in the Vineyard of the Lord: A Resource for Guiding the Development of Lay Ecclesial Ministry. Washington, DC: United States Conference of Catholic Bishops, 2005.

Crux: Taking the Catholic Pulse, January 30, 2017.

Dovre, Paul, ed. *The Future of Religious College*. Grand Rapids: Eerdmans, 2002.

Eck, Diana. *A New Religious America: How a "Christian Country" Has Become the World's Most Religiously Diverse Nation*. New York: HarperCollins, 2001.

Ellingson, Stephen. *Megachurch: Remaking Religious Tradition in the Twenty-First Century*. Chicago: University of Chicago Press, 2007.

Friedman, Thomas L. *Thank You for Being Late*. New York: Farrar, Straus, and Giroux, 2016.

Goldberg, Paul. "The Gospel of Church Architecture, Revised." *New York Times*, April 20, 1995. http://www.nytimes.com/1995/04/20/garden/the-gospel-of-church-architecture-revised.html?pagewanted=all.

Gordon, Ernest B. *Adoniram Judson Gordon: A Biography, with Letters and Illustrative Extracts Drawn from Unpublished or Uncollected Sermons and Addresses*. New York: Fleming H. Revell, 1896.

Graham, Stephen R. "Christian Hospitality and Pastoral Practices in a Multifaith Society: An ATS Project, 2010–2012." *Theological Education* 47, no. 1 (2012): 9.

————. *Reflections for the Meeting of "The Current State of Interfaith Education in the United States."* New York: Henry Luce Foundation, 2015.

Green, Emma. "How Will Young People Choose Their Religion?" *Atlantic*, March 20, 2016. https://www.theatlantic.com/politics/archive/2016/03/how-will-young-people-choose-their-religion/474366/.

Greer, Rowan. *Anglican Approaches to Scripture from the Reformation to the Present*. New York: Crossroads, 2006.

Gritsch, Eric W., and Robert W. Jenson. *Lutheranism*. Philadelphia: Fortress, 1976.

Hadaway, C. Kirk. *New Facts on Episcopal Church Growth and Decline*. New York: Domestic and Foreign Missionary Society, 2015.

Hall, Douglas John. *Thinking the Faith: Christian Theology in a North American Context*. Minneapolis: Augsburg, 1989.

Han, Sang-Ehil, Paul Louis Metzger, and Terry C. Muck. "Christian Hospitality and Pastoral Practice from an Evangelical Perspective." *Theological Education* 47, no. 1 (2012): 11–32.

Heclo, Hugh. *On Thinking Institutionally*. Boulder: Paradigm, 2008.

Heille, Gregory, OP. *The Preaching of Pope Francis: Missionary Discipleship and the Ministry of the Word*. Collegeville, PA: Liturgical, 2015.

Hendrix, Scott. *Recultivating the Vineyard: The Reformation Agendas of Christendom*. Louisville: John Knox, 2004.

Herzberg, Will. *Protestant, Catholic, Jew: An Essay in American Religious Sociology*. Garden City, NY: Doubleday, 1955.

Hess, Mary. "The Pastoral Practice of Christian Hospitality as Presence in Muslim-Christian Engagement: Contextualizing the Classroom." *Theological Education* 47, no. 2 (2013): 7–12.

Hofstadter, Richard. *Anti-intellectualism in American Life*. New York: Vintage Books, 1963.

Hout, Michael, and Tom W. Smith. *Fewer Americans Affiliate with Organized Religions, Belief and Practice Unchanged: Key Findings from the 2014 General Social Survey*. Chicago: NORC, 2015.

Ivereigh, Austin. *The Great Reformer: Francis and the Making of a Radical Pope*. New York: Henry Holt, 2014.

Jiwa, Munir. "Islamic Studies in the Interreligious Context of the Graduate Theological Union." Paper presented at meeting on Critical Issues in Interreligious Education in the United States, Graduate Theological Union, Berkeley, California, March 21–23, 2017.

Jodock, Darrell. "The Third Path, Religious Diversity, and Civil Discourse." In *The Vocation of Lutheran Higher Education*, edited by Jason Mahn. Edina, MN: Lutheran University Press, 2016.

Kääriäinen, Jukka A. "Mission." In *Gift and Promise: The Augsburg Confession and the Heart of Christian Theology*, edited by Edward H. Schroeder, Ronald Neustadt, and Stephen Hitchcock. Minneapolis: Fortress, 2016.

———. *Mission Shaped by Promise: Lutheran Missiology Confronts the Challenge of Religious Pluralism*. Eugene, OR: Wipf and Stock, 2012.

Kärkkäinen, Veli-Matti. *A Constructive Christian Theology for the Pluralistic World*. 5 vols. Grand Rapids: Eerdmans, 2013.

Kreimer, Nancy Fuchs. "Interreligious Education at Reconstructionist Rabbinical College: Thirty Years of Experiments, Exploration, and Evolution." Presented at meeting on Critical Issues in Interreligious Education in the United States, Graduate Theological Union, Berkeley, California, March 21–23, 2017.

Kujawa-Holbrook, Sheryl. "Worship, Music, and Generational Conflict." *Looking Forward: Theological Education, Young Adults, and the 21st-Century Church* 32, no. 2. http://www.faithformationlearningexchange.net/uploads/5/2/4/6/52 46709/young_adults__21st_century_church.pdf.

Labberton, Mark, ed. *Still Evangelical? Insiders Reconsider Political, Social, and Theological Meaning*. Downers Grove, IL: IVP, 2018.

Lipsey, Roger. "Abstraction—a Religious Art, Sometimes." In *An Art of Our Own: The Spiritual in Twentieth Century Art*, 1–28. Boston: Shambhala, 1988.

———. "What Is the Spiritual in Art." In *An Art of Our Own: The Spiritual in Twentieth Century Art*, 1–28. Boston: Shambhala, 1988.

Luther, Martin. "Ninety-Five Theses." In *Martin Luther's Basic Theological Writings*, edited by Timothy F. Lull. Minneapolis: Fortress, 1989.

MacIntyre, Alasdair. *After Virtue*. 2nd ed. Notre Dame: University of Notre Dame Press, 1981.

Madsen, Richard. *China and Christianity: Burdened Past, Hopeful Future*. Armonk, NY: M. E. Sharpe, 2001.

McConnell, Douglas. "Educating Seminarians for Convicted Civility in a Multifaith World." *Teaching Theology & Religion* 16, no. 4 (October 2013): 329–37.

McCurley, Foster R., ed. *Social Ministry in the Lutheran Tradition*. Minneapolis: Fortress, 2008.

Mead, Loren. *The Once and Future Church*. Washington, DC: Alban Institute, 1991.

Mikva, Rachel. "Reflections in the Waves: How Feminist/Womanist/ Mujerista Theory Informs the Pedagogy of Interreligious Studies." Presented at meeting on Critical Issues in Interreligious Education in the United States, Graduate Theological Union, Berkeley, California, March 21–23, 2017.

Mouw, Richard J. *Uncommon Decency: Christian Civility in an Uncivil World*. Rev. and exp. ed. Downers Grove, IL: IVP, 2010.

Mouw, Richard J., and Robert L. Millet, eds. *Talking Doctrine: Mormons and Evangelicals in Conversation*. Downers Grove, IL: InterVarsity, 2015.

Muck, Terry, and Frances S. Adeney. *Christianity Encountering World Religions: The Practice of Mission in the Twenty-First Century*. Grand Rapids: Baker Academic, 2009.

Newbigin, Lesslie. *Proper Confidence*. Grand Rapids: Eerdmans, 1995.

Newman, John Henry. *The Idea of a University*. New York: Rinehart, 1960.

Noll, Mark A. "The Divine Doctor" [interview with Jaroslav Pelikan], *Christianity Today* 34, no. 12 (1990): 26.

Orsi, Robert A. *Between Heaven and Earth: The Religious Worlds People Make and the Scholars Who Study Them*. Princeton: Princeton University Press, 2005.

Patel, Eboo. *Interfaith Leadership: A Primer*. Boston: Beacon Press, 2016.

Peace, Jennifer Howe. "Religious Self, Religious Other: Coformation as a Model for Interreligious Education." Paper presented at meeting on Critical Issues in Interreligious Education in the United States, Graduate Theological Union, March 21–23, 2017.

Pettegree, Andrew. *Brand Luther*. New York: Penguin Books, 2016.

Pierce, Elinor. "Beyond Common Ground: The Pluralism Project at Harvard University." Paper presented at meeting on the Current State of Interreligious Education in the United States, at the Henry Luce Foundation, September 21, 2015.

Pohl, Christine. *Making Room: Recovering Hospitality as a Christian Tradition*. Grand Rapids: Eerdmans, 1999.

Preus, James Samuel. *From Shadow to Promise*. Cambridge, MA: Belknap, 1969.

Price, Charles, and Louis Weil. *Liturgy for Living*. New York: Seabury, 1979.

Reisacher, Evelyne A. *Joyful Witness in the Muslim World: Sharing the Gospel in Everyday Encounters*. Grand Rapids: Baker Academic, 2016.

Ringenberg, William. *The Christian College: A History of Protestant Higher Education in America*. Grand Rapids: Eerdmans, 1984.

Saidi, Farida. "A Study of Current Leadership Styles in the North African Church." PhD diss., Fuller Theological Seminary, School of Intercultural Studies, 2010.

Sanneh, Lamin. *Translating the Message: The Missionary Impact on Culture*. Maryknoll, NY: Orbis Books, 1989.

Schuth, K. *Seminary Formation: Recent History, Current Circumstances, New Directions.* Collegeville, PA: Liturgical, 2016.

Scully, J. Eileen. "Theological Education for the Anglican Communion: The Promises and Challenges of TEAC." *Anglican Theological Review* 90, no. 2 (Spring 2008): 217.

Selingo, Jeffrey J. *College (Un)bound: The Future of Higher Education and What It Means for Students.* Boston: New Harvest, 2013.

Smith, Wilfred Cantwell. *Towards a World Theology: Faith and the Comparative History of Religion.* Philadelphia: Westminster, 1981.

Sparks, Allister, and Mpho Tutu. *Tutu Authorized.* Auckland, New Zealand: PQ Blackwell, 2011.

Spretnak, Charlene. "1945 to the Present—Allusive Spirituality." In *Spiritual Dynamic in Modern Art: Art History Reconsidered, 1800 to the Present.* New York: Palgrave Macmillan, 2014.

Sunquist, Scott W. *Understanding Christian Mission: Participation in Suffering and Glory.* Grand Rapids: Baker Academic, 2013.

Sykes, Stephen W. *The Integrity of Anglicanism.* London: Mowbray, 1978.

Tennent, Timothy C. *Christianity at the Religious Roundtable: Evangelicalism in Conversation with Hinduism, Buddhism, and Islam.* Grand Rapids: Baker Academic, 2001.

Tranvik, Mark D., trans. *The Freedom of a Christian.* Minneapolis: Augsburg, 2008.

Vaccari, Peter. "The Culture of Encounter: The Future of Seminary Formation." In *Seminary Formation: Recent History, Current Circumstances, New Directions,* by K. Schuth, 164–73. Collegeville, PA: Liturgical, 2016.

Valkenburg, Pim. "Learning with and from Religious Others." *Teaching Theology & Religion* 16, no. 4 (October 2013): 391.

Wells, Samuel. "How Common Worship Forms Local Character." *Studies in Christian Ethics* 15, no. 1 (2002): 67. journals.sagepub.com/doi/pdf/10.1177/095394680201500106.

Whiteman, Darrell. "Anthropology and Mission: An Incarnational Connection." *International Journal of Frontier Missions* 21, no. 2 (Summer 2004): 79–88.

Wuthnow, Robert. *The Restructuring of American Religion.* Princeton: Princeton University Press, 1988.

Yeh, Allen. *Polycentric Missiology: Twenty-First Century Mission from Everyone to Everywhere.* Downers Grove, IL: IVP Academic, 2016.

Yong, Amos. *Beyond the Impasse: Toward a Pneumatological Theology of Religions.* Eugene, OR: Wipf and Stock, 2014.

INDEX